Herbs

Jack Harvey

P9-CBF-478

An *ideals* Publication
First Printing
ISBN 0-89542-903-9 295

Consultant
Herbert F. Lamp
Professor of Biology
Northeastern Illinois University

Library of Congress Catalog Number: 80-65264

Published by Ideals Publishing Corporation
11315 Watertown Plank Road
Milwaukee, WI 53226

First published
Macdonald Educational Ltd.
Holywell House, Worship Street,
London EC2A 2EN

Contents

What do you know about herbs?

What do you know about herbs? Most people think at once of the jars and boxes of dried herbs sold in all supermarkets. Gift shops also sell them in matching sets with decorative labels. Almost everyone is also aware that herbs provide scent. Soaps, perfumes, and powders have pictures of fern, lavender, or lilies of the valley on their wrappers.

Among the hundreds of plants that make the world smell sweeter is garden mint. The most usual species is called spearmint. Like horseradish, it is grown on a large scale and sold in bottles as a sauce for meat. But peppermint is more important commercially. It contains menthol, an oil that flavors delicious, tooth-rotting chocolates, and gums. It also adds a special tang to some cigarettes.

Other smokers have a taste for "herbal" tobacco, made from the dried leaves of coltsfoot, betony and eyebright. But all tobacco is made from dried leaves. So even a Havana cigar is an "herbal" mixture.

Cures and curses

Most people are also aware that herbs were once used as medicine. Probably they think of these old remedies as part of a vanished rural way of life. White-coated chemists in gleaming laboratories have made them unnecessary. The truth is that herbal doctors still treat patients successfully. Moreover the great drug companies depend on plants for many other cures, from the menthol that clears a blocked nose, to the morphine that kills the pain of a serious illness.

The ability of herbs to kill or cure seems half magical, even to the rational minds of modern people. It is not surprising, therefore, that a knowledge of the power of plants has always been linked with the witch, witch doctor, and priest. Even the names of the herbs they used sound menacing: "hemlock, henbane, adder's tongue, nightshade, moonwort, leppardsbane." These poetic lines from a 16th century play list some of the deadliest poisons in the hedgerow. Bane is an old word meaning "That which causes ruin or woe"; and what was bad for the hens and leopards certainly did no good to a witch's enemy.

The meaning of the word

A word with so many uses is hard to define. *Herba* was the Latin word for grass. In this book the word herb is used to describe any plant whose root, stem, leaf, flower or seed serves to flavor other foods and is not eaten on its own. Oriental spices are included. The flowerbuds called cloves and the fruits of the pepper vine are as truly herbs as any less exotic flavorings.

The word *herb* also covers medicinal plants and those used in cosmetics or as coloring agents. Finally come plants that are infused, whether to make elderflower wine, nettle beer, or a nonalcoholic pot of tea.

▶ *Latin names are used to avoid the confusion that arises from the different names given to the same plant in different areas. The dandelion is labeled* Taraxacum officinale. *A capital letter is given to the* genus, *or group, to which the plant belongs. The species name is not given a capital. In the case of garden plants, there may also be a third name for varieties within a species.*

The dandelion is one of the most common of the plants that can be classed as herbs. Almost every part of the plant is useful in some way.

Dandelion wine can be made from the flowers. There are many recipes. A gallon of flowers is needed for each gallon of wine.

Leaves and stems can be chopped into a salad or made into a medicinal tea. It is said to ease stiff joints and relieve indigestion.

A tasty coffee can be made from the roasted roots of dandelion. An infusion of raw root is reputed to be good for some liver complaints.

Herbs and the ancients

Early humans, like the apes, were largely vegetarians. On their home ground, they probably retained the wild animal's instinct for avoiding food that was harmful to them. But as they developed the skills of weapon-making, trapping, and cooking, people began to hunt over ever wider territories. These meat-eaters still ate wild herbs, but they were no longer so familiar with herbs; and the results must sometimes have been fatal.

Because of both their immense benefits and great dangers, plants appeared in many primitive religious myths. These myths were created to account for the cycle of the seasons and other mysteries of life. They were not written down until much later; yet they provide us with clues to the workings of the primitive mind.

The all-powerful herb

In the early literature of all societies, there is a belief in the divine magic of herbs. Heracles gave the gods of Olympus victory over the Titans when he gave them the "herb of invulnerability." In the Old Testament, Rachel, Jacob's barren wife, was at last able to bear him a son with the aid of mandrakes, sold to her by her stepson Reuben. In India the Vedic gods became immortal by drinking an herbal brew called Soma. Other histories record the remarkable properties attributed to herbs.

Herbs and human sacrifice

A human sacrifice was often made in ancient times to hasten the arrival of

Herbal myths

Herbs were part of the religious magic of many civilizations, and often figure among their legends. Typical of these is the 5,000-year-old story of Gilgamesh and the "herb of immortality." Gilgamesh was king of Uruk on the Euphrates. His mother was a goddess, but his father was human. He and his friend Enkidu went on a long journey to the "land of the cedars" and killed a giant "whose jaws are death itself."

After the death of Enkidu, Gilgamesh went on a solitary search for eternal life. He met a man called Utnapishtim who spoke of an herb, buried deep in the ocean, that would give a man back his lost youth. Gilgamesh found the "herb of immortality." But as soon as he came ashore, a serpent stole it from him. The hero at last understood that one day he would have to die.

The life and death of the seasons is celebrated in the Greek myth of Persephone. The daughter of the corn goddess, Demeter, was abducted by the god of the underworld while picking poppies. Thereafter she spent all winter in a death-like sleep, probably induced by the narcotic power of the poppy.

spring. In Assyria, the god Tammuz died yearly and was brought back to life by Ishtar, the Mother Goddess. The Greeks knew Tammuz by his title Adonis, or Lord. The pheasant's eye anemone (*Adonis annua*) owes its Latin name to him; his blood was said to have turned it scarlet. It has been used to treat heart conditions.

The Tollund Man was another sacrificial victim. His 2,000-year-old corpse was found in a Danish peat bog. It was so well preserved that the contents of his stomach could be analyzed. His final meal included gold of pleasure, fat hen, black bindweed, and the wild pansy (The pansy, also featured in many medieval love potions used by black and white witches, is a slight narcotic). It seems clear that this meal was not typical of the tribe's diet; they are known to have been meat eaters. The recipe must have been prepared as part of the ritual of sacrifice.

The people who killed the Tollund man spent their lives producing their daily food. But in the sacrificial meal, they looked back to a time before they cultivated crops or kept livestock. Wild herbs had then been their principal source of food.

Supermarket hunters

The lives of modern people are quite different. The ability to hunt animals or identify a health-giving herb is no longer important to them. Specialists produce the food, and everyone else is free to enjoy other occupations. People often no longer know how their food is produced or what processes it undergoes before they buy it.

The wild herbs that gave our ancestors food, medicine, and a basis for their religious life, are now regarded as weeds. Chemical sprays and a swelling population leave fewer places where wild plants can grow. There has been a recent revival of interest in herbs and spices, but primarily to improve the taste of over-refined foods. In earlier times herbs were an important part of humankind's relationship to the universe in which they lived.

◀ *Today, people hunt for their food on the shelves and in the freezers of the local supermarket. How many of those who regularly eat packaged sage and onion stuffing would recognize a sage plant if they saw it growing?*

7

Ancient herbalists

Some of the earliest books were written by herbalists. The herbal of the Chinese Emperor Sheng Noong is said to date from 2,700 B.C. In Egypt, around the same time, there were 2,000 herbal doctors. They treated their patients with careful doses of poisons from the poppy and the autumn crocus. In India the Ayurvedic school of medicine used a list of 700 herbs; even more were known to the Assyrians.

Hippocrates is often called the "Father of Medicine." The Hippocratic oath still governs a doctor's standard of behavior. Hippocrates, born in 477 B.C., frequently prescribed herbs, including absinthe and tarragon. He suggested rue and garlic to ease the pains of childbirth.

The most detailed account of Roman herbalism comes in Pliny's *Natural History.* Eight of the 37 volumes are devoted to medicinal plants. Pennyroyal is suggested for a fever, basil as an aphrodisiac, and sow thistles to sweeten the breath.

The great doctors of the age were both Greeks. The names of Dioscorides and Galen cast a spell over herbalism for 1,500 years. Galen, physician to Marcus Aurelius, treated cramps with rhubarb imported from China. Two favorite remedies used by Dioscorides, who served in Nero's army, were lavender and licorice root. He even claimed that an amulet of heliotrope worn during sexual intercourse would prevent conception.

How herbs got their names

The names of herbs such as pilewort, birthwort and goutwort, all advertise their old usefulness. The word *wort* means "a plant that is used for." Other herbs owe their names

Avicenna was one of the great philosophers of the Middle Ages. He was a Muslim, but his medical encyclopedia was quoted with respect by both Jews and Christians. The school of medicine at Salerno University, in Southern Italy, was largely based on Islamic herbalism. Avicenna devised an unlikely contraceptive; it required the woman to drink two liters (almost two quarts) of brewed basil.

▶ *According to Greek mythology, the god Apollo tried to rape a nymph called Daphne, but the earth mother saved her by changing her into a bay laurel. Apollo, who was also god of poetry, consoled himself by weaving a coronet from her leaves. Thereafter poets were crowned with bay leaves and the Latin name for bay became* Laurus nobilis. *The name Daphne is now borne by a group of nonedible shrubs.*

to mythology. Iris was the "many-colored messenger of the gods," and elecampane takes its Latin name *Inula helenium* from Helen of Troy. Sage bears the Latin name *Salvia officinalis* because of its healing powers. *Officinalis* as a species name indicates that it was once sold in apothecary shops.

Herbalism and astrology

The ancients were convinced of the connection between herbs and the stars. Plants grew and died with the seasons, just as stars and planets wandered through the sky. Ancient Assyrian priests plotted these heavenly movements with great accuracy. As late as 1650,

▲ *The witch used herbs to cure the sick, but because of her knowledge and power she was feared. Witches may also have used narcotic herbs, which made them think they could fly.*

the herbalist Nicholas Culpeper said, "All men are unfit to be physicians, who are not artists in astrology."

The Doctrine of Signatures

Herbal prescription was made more complicated by the belief in the Doctrine of Signatures, a treatise that stated that the healing virtues of plants could be discerned from their appearance. The parallel veins on plantain leaves looked like human ribs and so were used to cure rheumatism. Scarlet pimpernel, burdock, and red clover — being red — were said to be good for purifying the blood. Agrimony and celandine had yellow flowers, so they were used to relieve jaundice. Pliny said that herbs growing on the heads of statues would stop a headache.

Herbal magic

A belief in the magical power of herbs was a natural reaction to the speedy death or blissful hallucination that can result from eating a few leaves or berries. *The Golden Ass* is a delightful novel, written in ancient Rome, that illustrates the awe in which a person who understood herbs was held.

The hero falls in love with a witch's servant. Each night the witch eats herbs that turn her into an owl. Having seen her fly, the hero begs his beloved to steal some herbs for him. By mistake she turns him into a donkey. Only after many perilous adventures does he succeed in regaining his human shape by munching rose petals.

The rose was always a sign of spiritual purity. Angelica and mallow also supposedly offered protection against witchcraft. Too, the wild garlic, which still encircles the ruins of many old monasteries, was planted there to fend off the devil.

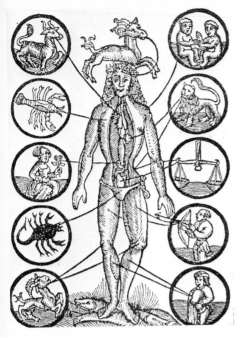

▲ Each part of the body came under the domination of a zodiacal sign. Each herb was also governed by a planet. Mustard, for example, was a herb of Mars. When Mars was in Aries, mustard was said to purge the brain, but when the planet was in Scorpio, the same herb stirred up lust.

The plant most used for evil purposes was mistletoe growing on a hawthorn bush. Mistletoe is more revered than almost any other plant. Pliny said that it would cure epilepsy. It was sacred to the Druids when found on an oak tree, for they believed that whatever grew on an oak tree was sent from heaven. It is also sacred to the Ainu of northern Japan, but they hope to find it on a willow, which is their tree of life.

The Christmas kiss under the mistletoe is a survival of old Nordic fertility rites. The white fruits of the mistletoe appear when all nature seems dead; the midwinter rite was believed to encourage dormant plants to come back to life. A kiss symbolizes human fertility.

▼ This medieval illustration shows a dog tied to the stem of a mandrake. The human-shaped root of the mandrake was said to shriek when disturbed, causing those who heard it to go mad or die. So herbalists tied a dog to the stem to uproot the herb.

11

The physic garden

During the Middle Ages, the great herb gardens were cultivated by monks, and it was the brothers and sisters in religious houses who set up hospitals and cared for the sick. Plants known to the Greeks, Druids, and Anglo-Saxons continued to be cultivated for their medicinal powers, despite the pagan superstition attached to so many of them. Louis the Pious, son of the Emperor Charlemagne, drew up a long list of plants that was to be grown on his lands. Parsley, chives, sage, and most other modern culinary herbs were evidently appreciated in the ninth century. Among the Royal medicinal herbs were marshmallow, feverfew, and spurge.

Today, people tend to look back with horror to the brutal methods of surgery that existed in the Middle Ages. But it is wrong to think that there were no pain killers. A soporific sponge was inhaled by the patient before amputations. It was soaked in the juices of opium, henbane, hemlock, mandrake, and ivy. These contain poisons that kill pain very effectively — and kill the patient if overprescribed. The sponge was invented by the Chinese and brought to Europe by the Arabs.

In the twelfth century, the abbess Hildegarde of Bingen and Abbot Alexander Neckam of the Austinian Abbey at Cirencester, both wrote knowledgeably about herbs and their uses. Early in the 14th century Pietro de' Crescenzi wrote a book on gardens for the King of Naples. He describes the beauty of fountains surrounded by low hedges of rue, sage, marjoram, and mint.

▼ *Guy de Chaulliac directs the planting of herbs and the grinding of drugs. He was one of the foremost doctors of his time. He trained at Bologna, later taught at Montpelier, and during the Black Death was surgeon to the Pope, who then lived in exile at Avignon.*

▲ Hyssop "Doth comfort benummed sinews and joints."

had, in fact, been copied straight from earlier manuscripts. The results are often charming to look at, but misleading.

One exception is the herbal by Otto Brunfels (1464-1534), which was published in Strasbourg. The drawings reflect acute observation. Two other herbals circulated widely on the continent. One was by Mathias de L'Obel, who was born in Flanders but died in London. The other was by Leonard Fuchs. Both are immortalized in the names of showy garden flowers, the lobelia and the fuchsia.

The fine engravings in Fuchs' work were copied in William Turner's herbal, one of the first to be printed in England. Turner was Dean of Wells and was embroiled in the religious conflicts that followed the dissolution of the monasteries by Henry VIII. His book, *The names of herbes* and those by Thomas Hyll and John Gerard, which soon followed, helped to preserve the plant lore accrued by medieval monks.

Herb-surrounded fountains remained popular with the Italians. Early descriptions of the magnificent gardens of the Villa D'Este at Tivoli speak of lavender hedges enclosing marjoram, hyssop, and other green herbs. The herbs have now gone, leaving only the glorious fountains.

The herbal in print

The invention of printing coincided with a revival of interest in the ancient Greeks and Romans. Books on herbs must have had a great appeal for the Renaissance mind; they were published in large numbers. Galen and Dioscorides, Aristotle and Hippocrates were quoted on almost every page. Many illustrations display a scant knowledge of plants and

▲ Rue: "The poets say it is good for the head, eyes, breast, liver, heart and spleen."

Turner said that his ambition was "To know and see the herbes myself," and he traveled widely. Gerard's knowledge was less profound, but his herbal of 1597 was an immense success. Although its text was based on a translation from a work by Rembert Dodoens and its pictures came from a German publication, Gerard's work showed enthusiasm and plenty of good sense.

The 1,600 pages of Gerard's *Herball* are a mixture of credulity and practical gardening. (Besides being a surgeon, Gerard was in charge of Lord Burleigh's gardens in London and at Theobalds). He takes a patriotic delight in refuting the Greek Galen's idea that Solomon's Seal should never be taken internally. Ingenious persons in Hampshire, he says, drink the infused roots to mend broken bones. On the subject of egg plant, he writes, "I rather wish Englishmen to content themselves with the meat and sauce of their own country."

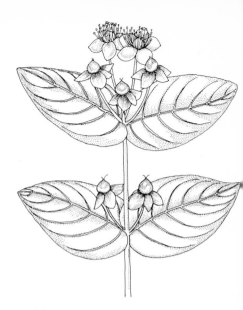

▲ *Tutsan: "The leaves heal broken shins and scabbed legs."*

Parkinson and Culpeper

The most influential herbals of the 17th century were both the work of apothecaries. John Parkinson dedicated his first book to Queen Henrietta Maria and his next to Charles I. The first has a large section on herbs. The second is subtitled "A universalle and compleate Herball." He prescribed valerian for "those that are troubled with a cough" and primroses to relieve a headache. He also says that hens will lay better in winter if fed on hemp. He does not describe what effect the eggs will have on those who eat them.

Nicholas Culpeper was another apothecary who lived in England in the 17th century. His herbal is partly an attempt to sell the produce of his London garden. His advertisement for herbal medicines is very readable and has often been reprinted, right up to modern times. Astrology is important in his prescriptions, and sometimes he is guilty of inventing links between herbs and planets.

▲ *Mugwort "Breaks the stone."*

William Coles, whose *Art of Simpling* was published in 1656, scorned the idea that plants were governed by the stars. "Herbs are more antient than the sunne or moon or starres, they being created on the fourth day, whereas plants were the third." A sincere belief in the book of Genesis was, unfortunately, no more scientific than Culpeper's astrology.

The four humors

One belief was shared by all the herbalists of the Renaissance. This was Hippocrates' doctrine of the four humors. Physical and mental behavior were said to be caused by phlegm, blood, black bile, and yellow bile. Respectively the humors were cold and wet, hot and wet, cold and dry, hot and dry. Depending on their balance, a person

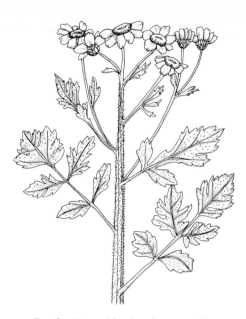

▲ Feverfew "Is good for them that are giddie in the head, or which have the turning called vertigo."

▲ Ranunculus repens: "Hang in linen cloth about the neck of lunatics in the waning period of the moon."

was either phlegmatic (slothful), sanguine (full of lust and energy), melancholy (given to brooding), or choleric (bad tempered). Herbs were also said to be hot, cold, wet, or dry. To restore a healthy balance, one had to purge the body of any excess of a humor.

Plaintain was cold and dry in the second degree. According to Parkinson, three roots boiled in wine would cure the tertian ague. A quartain ague needed four roots. The mathematics are based on the three- and four-day cycles of the two fevers. Capsicum, the red or green pepper, was measured as hot and dry in the fourth degree. This fruit "out of the new found world" was good "for them that be of cold complexion." Saffron was hot in the second degree and dry in the first. Turner blended it with poppy juice, milk, and rose oil to ease "payne of the fete."

15

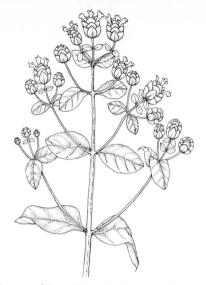

▲ *Dittany of Crete "Draweth thornes out of the feet."*

Some complaints recur in the herbals with alarming frequency. Parkinson recommends sweet marjoram "Against the poison of venemous beasts." Basil is, "good for the stryking of a se dragon." Was that a jellyfish? Wormwood, southernwood, vervain, and a hundred other herbs were suggested to expel worms.

The dreaded plague

The herbalists were kept busy by recurrent epidemics. The Black Death of 1348 and the frequent outbreaks of bubonic plague that occurred were caused by flea-infected rats. The victims suffered agonizing swellings in the groin and under the arms. Thousands died. Herbalists were as confused as their wretched patients. One recalled that Galen had chewed rue to avoid infection. Another made pills containing hellebore and opium. A third applied a hot onion to the tumors, having first stuffed the onion with rue, fig, and Venice Treakle. The Treakle was a compound of 61 herbs and spices and was one of

▶ *The Garden of Fidelity was one of ten gardens made at Kabul by the Mongul Emporer Babur, who ruled the Muslim Empire of Northern India in the 16th century. Babur loved music, but flowers were his passion. He ordered his gardeners to plant borders filled with sweet scented herbs.*

Venice's most profitable exports. Tobacco was another hopeless remedy; even small children were obliged to smoke. Inhaling sweet-scented pomanders and posies was also tried, since bad air was thought to cause epidemics.

In Italy *mal aria,* bad air, became the name for the fever known earlier as tertian ague. A bouquet of rosemary or the fumitory prescribed by John of Milan were both useless against the anopheles mosquito. But many of the herbalists' cures did work, even if their methods were haphazard and their explanations fanciful.

▲ **Tulipa silvestris:** *"With red wine, for them that have crick in the neck."*

16

درختهای انار هست هم هست کرد اکرد حوض تمام سبزه زار

جای عین باغ همین است در وقت زرد شدن بهار بسیار

A fortune from the herbs

From the earliest days of sea travel, herbs and spices were among the most important items of trade. More than 3,000 years ago, Queen Hatsepsut of Egypt imported myrrh from Somalia to put into her cosmetics, and the ancient Babylonians knew most of the oriental spices. Cinnamon, cloves, and ginger were in their medicines, as well as their food. Alexander's invasion of Asia in 333 B.C. gave the Greeks five times as many spices as they had known before.

Pepper was at first a costly medicine, but by the time of the Roman Empire it was essential in cooking. The price was always high, and the condiment often became a form of currency. The Gothic invaders of Italy in the fifth century demanded 3,000 lbs of pepper as part of the price for not sacking Rome. Venetian galleys supplied the European spice market during the Middle Ages. Cane sugar first came to the West at this time. Like pepper, its first use was in medicine, and it was centuries before it became a popular food.

The cup that cheers

The Italians who first found America were looking for new routes to the profitable

▲ *Peppercorns are the dried fruits of the vine* Piper nigrum. *White pepper is made by removing the dark outer husks. Areca nut trees, or other profitable crops, often support the vines.*

▲ *The clove tree can be seven meters tall. It produces 34 kilos of flower buds each year, which are dried in the sun. The spikey clove takes its name from the French* clou, *meaning "nail."*

An 18th century English family at tea. They are shown surrounded by symbols of prosperity and social position. Tea had to be transported all the way from the Chinese port of Canton; only the well-to-do could afford to drink it. The finer blends were outrageously costly, and even the cheapest quality carried an exorbitant tax. The cups and saucers are fine porcelain, also imported from China. At this period, tea cups still had no handles. The family silver is, however, of European design.

spices of the East. Their voyages of discovery introduced the European palate to many new flavors. Chocolate was the drink of the Aztec kings, and they flavored it with vanilla. Some taxes were even paid to them in cocoa beans. The popularity of chocolate spread to Spain and from there to all the capitals of Europe. People met in chocolate houses to gossip and flirt over a mug of the exotic new beverage. It was denounced from the pulpit as an inflamer of passions and corrupter of morals. But Linnaeus must have felt more kindly towards it, for he gave it the name *Theobroma cacao*, which means "food of the gods."

Coffee houses also became popular meeting places in the 17th century, and coffee, too, was denounced from the pulpit. But one enthusiast, J. S.Bach, wrote a sprightly cantata in praise of the drink. Coffee originally grew wild in Ethiopia but is now cultivated most intensively in South America. Mexican chocolate is now mainly grown on the west coast of Africa, and the Mexican vanilla is grown primarily in the Seychelles.

War in a teacup

Lu Yu, a Chinese philosopher of the eighth century, wrote a lengthy treatise on the delights of tea. "It is better than wine," he said, "for it does not lead to intoxication." But the Chinese were slow to share their drink with the outside world.

In the late 17th century, the British were allowed to set up trading posts in Canton. They more than paid for the tea by selling Indian-grown opium to the Chinese. The Chinese authorities tried to put a stop to this illegal traffic, and two wars resulted. Britain was victorious, but in the meantime tea had been found wild in northern India. Before long, Assam and Sri Lanka were producing most of the world's tea. Tea was now cheap and was popular with the working classes. One moralist denounced it as "an engenderer of effeminacy and laziness."

To supply the boom market, special fast ships were developed to bring the new season's tea to Europe. These elegant clippers carried up to 2,000 tons of cargo. They were superseded by steamships in the 1870's.

Spice island empires

All through history, trade has led to conquest and conquest to trade. Spices are light and highly concentrated, which makes them easy to transport. In the past, traders were able to ask high prices for them because they were rare and exotic. They often tried to prevent their customers from knowing where the spice trees were to be found. Herodotus was told that cinnamon grew in a jungle south of the Nile, guarded by ferocious birds. In fact it grew in Ceylon and was brought on rafts across the Indian Ocean to Madagascar and from there up to the Red Sea.

Arabs continued to supply the European market for another 2,000 years. Pepper, ginger, cinnamon, and cloves were sold to the Venetians in Alexandria. This trade was wiped out when the sea route to India was discovered in 1498.

Europeans fought one another and colonized Asia for its spices. The Dutch controlled the Moluccas in the 17th century. They forced up the price of cloves and nutmegs by limiting the number of trees grown in the "Spice Isles." Cloves are now grown in Zanzibar and ginger in Jamaica. Their prices have all fallen, and there is no longer a spice precious enough to ransom a great city.

1. Chocolate is made from the beans of the Cacao tree. It originally grew in Central America.

2. The Vanilla orchid is native to Central America.

6. Myrrh, the resin from the shrub *Commiphora myrrha,* was exported in biblical times from Somalia, where it still grows.

7. Frankincense, resin from the tree *Boswellia carterii,* has been produced in Somalia and Arabia for many thousands of years.

8. Pepper was originally found on the southwest coast of India. It still grows there, in Indonesia, and in Thailand.

9. Cinnamon, the inner bark of the tree *Cinnamomum zeylanicum,* is grown in Sri Lanka, India, and Indonesia.

3. Tea grew wild as a 30-foot tall tree in China, where it is still grown.

4. Coffee was first found in Ethiopia. The Arabs were the first to drink it.

5. Ginger is an East Asian native. The rhizomes are now cultivated by India, Jamaica, and Nigeria.

10. Nutmeg and mace grow on a tall evergreen. They are cultivated in the Moluccas and in the West Indies.

11. Cloves originate from the Moluccas. The unopened flower buds are gathered in Tanzania, Malaysia, and Indonesia.

12. Tobacco first came to Europe from Mexico. It is now grown in 80 countries, including the U.S.A., China, and India.

21

Drugs and distractions

Most human beings seem to need some form of drug to help them to relax. Alcohol, tobacco, and chewing gum are substances shared by millions; where they are not popular, there is always a local substitute. Psychologists offer various explanations for this need; but, whatever the cause, it is answered by a wide variety of herbal products.

South American Indians have chewed coca leaf for hundreds of years. The coca trees once grew in groves sacred to the sun, whose human image was the Inca. Chewing coca improves stamina and produces a general sense of well-being. An extract from the leaves is made into cocaine, which is inhaled through the nose. In the late 19th century Freud thought cocaine might cure certain mental disorders; but it proved too dangerous. The Indian version of coca is called betel. It is the leaf of *Piper betel,* a vine related to pepper. The leaf is wrapped around an areca nut before being chewed.

Australian aborigines also like to chew. They roast the twigs of a shrub called pituri, then pulp them with water, and mix them with other shredded leaves. Like coca, pituri has a distinct narcotic effect.

Smoking and chewing

After alcohol, too vast a subject to touch on, tobacco is the most widely-used herbal palliative. When it first reached Europe from America, it was believed to be a wonderful medicine. It was said to be especially good for the lungs and that it would cure chilblains. Soon it was simply enjoyed as a pleasant

habit, while non-smokers complained that it was dirty and smelly.

Tobacco is not only a good smoke, it can be sniffed. During the 18th century, snuff was more fashionable than pipes. Society men and women carried elegant little porcelain or silver boxes and sucked the dust up their nostrils from the crook of the thumb. Sailors and other less genteel people chewed tobacco. The habit seems to have died with the modern taboo against spitting.

▲ *The daughters of Louis XIV smoking. Pipes and cigars were at first the only ways of smoking. Respectable women usually only indulged in the habit when no men were present.*

Chewing gum comes from latex in the trunk of the sapodilla tree. Like rubber it is a native of South America. The huge demand for gum, coated with peppermint or spearmint-flavored sugar, has led to other related trees being tapped.

Tobacco and chewing gum both help to reduce tension, which is regarded as a major health hazard. However, chewing gum is said to be harmful to the teeth and to the digestion, and heavy smoking has now been proved beyond a doubt to lead to various forms of cancer. Even so, governments have always found the tobacco habit an easy way of raising taxes and continue to do so despite the campaign against smoking.

Cannabis and heroin

Indian hemp has been smoked and eaten for thousands of years in Asia and the Eastern Mediterranean. It was not thought to be a cause of ill-health or crime. Today the drug is illegal in countries that place no ban on alcohol, which is guilty on both counts. Government reports have tried to show a link between cannabis and crime, but they have only been able to do so by the kind of logic that says "All burglars carry handkerchiefs, therefore handkerchiefs cause crime." In countries where cannabis is illegal and its possession can lead to a prison sentence, it does tend to be used by people who are in other ways in conflict with society and its laws. But cannabis smoking is not addictive.

Heroin comes from opium and is injected straight into the blood stream. It is addictive. Fortunes are made by syndicates that smuggle opium, and addicts are often led into a life of crime by the high price they have to pay for their habit. Attempts have been made to prevent both coca and opium from being grown, but aside from being profitable to illegal operators, both have legitimate medicinal uses.

Opium is derived from the opium poppy. The juice is milked from the unripe seedhead and dried to become dark and gummy. Opium originated in the Middle East, but addiction was a problem in China even in the 13th century. Marco Polo quotes a Chinese proverb: "Don't stab your enemy in the back, give him some opium."

Murder in the hedgerows

There are plenty of delicious, health-giving plants to be found in the wild, and even on waste spaces in cities. But always be certain that you know what you are eating. Most wild plants are not poisonous, but some are; and a few are fatal, even in small doses.

Plants of the carrot family are particularly confusing. They have flat flower heads, like open umbrellas, and are known as umbellifers. Hemlock killed Socrates and could do the same to you if you eat it thinking it is wild fennel. The berries of bittersweet and black nightshade look good enough to eat. But these near relatives of the salad tomato can be fatal. And it is not for nothing that the autumn crocus is named after Colchis, home-town of the murderous witch Medea. A good reference book will help you to identify herbs. Examine picture and plant carefully. If in doubt — don't.

1. Deadly nightshade flowers in June on dry wasteland. The berries are attractive, but even one can be fatal. All parts are toxic.

2. White bryony flowers in July. All parts are toxic and the juice irritates the skin.

3. The berries and leaves of the yew tree are fatally poisonous. Trees used to be grown in church yards, away from livestock, to provide wood for medieval longbows.

4. Hemlock is common on waste land and near streams. Most poison is in the young leaves and unripe seeds.

5. Hemlock waterdropwort is common near water. The roots are especially dangerous.

6. Monkshood grows in shade. It flowers in June. All parts are fatal.

7. Henbane grows in dry, sandy places and flowers in July. All parts are toxic.

8. The autumn crocus is sometimes found wild. It flowers in September and has only leaves and seeds in spring. The corms and seeds are toxic.

The scientific case for herbs

Modern science has made a great difference to the ways in which herbs are used. The chemist likes to know exactly which substance in a plant is responsible for a particular effect. It is then possible to manufacture a synthetic compound that imitates the chemical structure of that substance. Synthetic drugs are preferred because they are more concentrated and it is easier to measure an accurate dose. Herbal treatments are sometimes still used, even though analysis has failed to isolate the beneficial principle. But they are prescribed because they work and not because Galen or Culpeper approved of them.

Mucilage dissolves in water and becomes slimy. It is present to some degree in most food plants and is an aid to their digestion. The herbaceous mulleins are rich in mucilage and can be used to treat irritations of the mouth and throat.

Alkaloids are nitrogenous substances and often poisonous. Some alkaloids are used as antispasmodics; some for liniments and ointments.

Medicinal properties

The scent and flavor in herbs are mainly due to volatile oils. These are not just fragrant and tasty; they are often of medicinal use. The thymol in thyme is an effective antiseptic. The oil in pennyroyal, rubbed on the skin, deters insects. Volatile oils also increase the action of the kidneys and the rate of perspiration. They are helpful in cleansing the system of impurities and infections.

Glycosides are complex substances, built up partly of sugars. Among the glycosides are the lather-producing saponins, which are present in many plants. The soapiest of all is soapwort (bouncing bet). The body is not able to absorb much of these substances, and they tend to act as laxatives and expectorants. Hellebores and several other wild plants contain glycosides that are poisonous.

Hyssop, angelica, and many other herbs contain tannins. These taste bitter and stimulate the digestive juices. They are valuable in the treatment of stomach complaints.

▲ *A modern herbal medicine, sold as a nerve sedative, contains mistletoe, valerian, and skullcap. All these plants have been known and used as sedatives for thousands of years.*

The story of aspirin

The leaves and twigs of white willow were used in antiquity to treat rheumatism. The cure was suggested by the Doctrine of Signatures. Since willows grow in damp places and rheumatism occurs because of damp, it seemed obvious that one would cure the other. In 1838 chemists found that the bark of white willow contains an acid, which they named salicylic acid. The same acid is also in the bark of birch trees and *spireas*. Fifty years later, Hermann Dreser made a synthetic version, which he called acetylsalicylic acid. This enormous name described the little white pain killer swallowed daily by millions all over the world. Its common name, aspirin, comes from *spireas*. So far, no better way has been found to relieve the pain of rheumatism.

Yesterday's medicine today

The aspirin is by no means the only modern medicine to owe its existence to prescientific herbalism. The earliest Chinese herbal specifies the use of chaulmoogra oil for the treatment of leprosy. The name of this wonderful drug was preserved down the centuries, but it was nearly always used to sell products that had no effect at all on the ravages of the disease. It was not until this century that the *Hydnocarpus* tree was identified. The oil it produces is believed to be one described by the emperor Sheng Noong. It has proved to be especially valuable in treating leprosy, when an early diagnosis has been made.

Wormwood, as its name suggests, is an age-old remedy for worms. A near relative of wormwood is now grown on a commercial scale in Iran and Turkestan for the manufacture of the modern remedy for roundworm.

Asian remedies

Ephedrine is an alkaloid extracted from the shrub *Ephedra sinica*. Asian doctors have been been prescribing parts of this plant for thousands of years to alleviate fevers and headaches. It operates on the nervous system and is produced under a variety of brand names in sprays and pills for asthma and hay fever. It can also be used to raise the blood pressure of some heart conditions. Its stimulating effect on the nervous system can result in insomnia.

The snakeroot is another modern wonder drug that was recognized by Hindu doctors at least 2,000 years ago. Western medicine has only recently discovered its value in treating psychiatric disorders. The alkaloid it contains is known as reserpine; it acts as an antidepressant.

Key
1. *Dill*
2. *Dandelion leaves*
3. *Kelp*
4. *Elderberries*
5. *Nettle*
6. *Cowslip*
7. *Elecampane*
8. *Fat hen*
9. *Sunflower seeds*
10. *Parsley*
11. *Rose hips*

Many herbs are rich in vitamins. Parsley and rose hips are two of the most concentrated sources of Vitamin C. The seeds of fat hen and sunflowers contain Vitamin B.

Vitamin A is to be found in cowslips, nettles, and elecampane. Most herbs also contain a variety of minerals. Parsley, dill, and kelp are especially rich in iron.

A healthy diet

Much of the benefit of herbs lies in the vitamins and minerals they contain. In the past century, scientists have learned a great deal about the importance of a healthy diet. Vitamins only began to be understood in the 1880s. It was discovered that in parts of the world where polished rice was the main food, the disease beriberi was likely to occur. The most typical symptom of the disease is the swollen belly so often seen in the victim of famine in underdeveloped countries. The health-giving ingredient that is removed from polished rice is now known as Vitamin B. The vitamin is in fact one of a group of twelve, all of which are necessary. Pellagra and pernicious anemia are two of the worst conditions that result from Vitamin B deficiencies.

▲ *The foxglove contains a powerful glycoside. The drug digitalis, containing this glycoside, is now one of the standard treatments for heart conditions. Foxgloves are grown commercially in Hungary and the Harz mountains to supply drug companies.*

Vitamins in herbs

The benefits of Vitamin C were recognized long before ascorbic acid had been isolated or given a name. Sailors on long sea voyages had always suffered from scurvy. During the 18th century, the captains of ships found that the disease cleared up if their men ate citrus fruits, particularly oranges and limes.

Vitamin C is present in the majority of herbs, parsley and rose hips being two of the richest sources. The body requires 30 to 40 milligrams of the vitamin every day, as it has no way of storing it. Some dieticians believe that massive doses of as much as ten grams will prevent colds and other infections.

Vitamins E and A are also to be found in herbs. They are both fat soluble, unlike B and C, which dissolve in water. Young nettle leaves and elecampane flowers can both contain Vitamin A. Vitamin E can be obtained from spinach and dandelion leaves.

The poisonous cure

The bark of a twining plant that grows in Guyana was used by the Indians to make a poison called curare. An arrow dipped in curare can paralyze a warm-blooded creature so that it dies in less than a minute and yet remains fit to eat. In modern medicine, this virulent poison has been used in the treatment of spastic paralysis and as an ingredient in shock therapy.

The foxglove was used by the old herbalists to treat epilepsy and scrofula ("the King's evil"). It also had a strong connection with witchcraft. There is no record that it was ever prescribed for heart disease, but the function of the heart was not then fully understood by herbalists. They may even have cured heart attacks with foxglove leaves without a proper diagnosis of the symptoms.

The modern understanding of the powers of the foxglove began in 1875. Dr. William Withering published a report on the herb's many medicinal virtues. His interest had been sparked by a cure for dropsy, taught to him by an old countrywoman in Shropshire. Dropsy is a disease that causes the body to swell up with excessive fluid. Foxglove tea increased the patient's output of urine and reduced the visible symptoms. Dr. Withering thought that the plant's diuretic function was what mattered. But he was wrong. What he did not realize was that dropsy can be caused by congestive heart failure. The main benefit of the foxglove was that it made the patient's blood circulate more efficiently.

Withering's service to medicine was in pointing others to the path of discovery. It was 150 years before digitalis was prescribed correctly. It is toxic, but it can be taken daily and has prolonged the lives of many millions of heart sufferers.

An herbal dressing

In World War I, sphagnum moss was used as a surgical dressing. It was applied on gauze to open wounds. It had twice the absorbency of any cotton batting then on the market; therefore, blood-soaked dressings did not have to be changed so often. This reduced the discomfort of the wounded and freed the nursing staff for other duties. Garlic, known for thousands of years as an antiseptic, was sometimes used with the moss to prevent infection.

The foxglove is not the only poisonous plant to give good service in the hospital and the doctor's office. Deadly nightshade and henbane produce atropine and scopalomine, which are used in shock therapy for schizophrenia and in the treatment of ulcers. Morphine is derived from the opium poppy and is the most effective of all pain killers. It is used judiciously by the medical profession because of its addictive tendencies. Other medicinal herbs are so harmless that they are included in lozenges, vapor rubs, cough medicines, and similar preparations. Myrrh, camphor, thymol, menthol, cinnamon, and eucalyptus oil offer mild but effective relief for colds.

The fever bark

Quinine is usually replaced by a synthetic drug nowadays, but for centuries it was the only known cure for malaria. It is made from the bark of the cinchona tree, which grows wild in Bolivia and Peru. The Indians had always used it to cure fevers and taught their Spanish conquerors to value it. But they would only sell them the bark and always refused to let them know where the trees grew. Spanish missionaries brought the drug to Europe and so it became known as "Jesuit's bark." At first conservative medical men stuck stubbornly to bloodletting, the treatment by which generations of doctors had killed off their patients. Then, slowly, the drug was accepted.

By the 19th century, quinine was in short supply. Europe's exploitation of her Asian colonies was hampered by malaria, but the South American Indians still held on to their secret. At last a Charles Ledger obtained seeds; cinchona trees took root in Java and Ceylon. Ledger's Aymara manservant was murdered by his people for giving his master the precious seeds. The tree's name, *Cinchona ledgeriana*, records Ledger's success.

Wonder drug of the future?

The results achieved by plants like the foxglove and deadly nightshade make it foolhardy to dismiss other "folk cures." Mistletoe was used as a cure for cancer over 2,000 years ago, and its uses as a possible cure for the disease is now being reinvestigated.

Of course many old herbal remedies only worked because the body has an amazing ability to cure itself, and the patient's mind was set at rest by the doctor's prescribing a sweet-or-foul-tasting potion. But many of the potions were tried and tested, and the fact that they have given way to synthetic drugs, does not diminish their value in the past.

The Asiatic belief in ginseng may be partly due to the fact that, like the mandrake, it has a root shaped roughly like a human being. But that root sells well at very high prices, which suggests that people feel better for taking it. Hundreds of acres in the Appalachian Mountains are devoted to the crop, which is exported to a hungry market in Hong Kong. But medical opinion is divided as to whether it is a cure-all or a cure-nothing. Reports from Russia suggest that it affects the workings of glands such as the pituitary, adrenals, and gonads; but further tests will be needed to convince sceptics. It is possible that science will one day uncover the secret power of this root, just as it did for the poppy and the willow.

◀ *Ginseng has for centuries been the Oriental panacea. It has recently been used in the U.S.S.R. to treat ulcers and heart conditions. Mental and physical performance are both said to be improved by taking it.*

Dyes and perfumes

Chemical dyes are only 125 years old. Before then all the color of clothes and furnishings came from plants. The range of these dyers' herbs was endless. In Scotland and Scandinavia, lichens were used, gathered from local rocks. With urine as a mordant, a rich variety of shades was possible. In other areas, dyers' herbs were grown as big business. Woad, saffron, and madder were all farmed commercially. There were still four woad farms in Lincolnshire, England, at the end of the last century.

Saffron has always been costly, as only the stigmas are used, and it takes 200,000 flowers to make a pound. Tumeric roots make a cheaper yellow.

Woad was the traditional blue dye in Europe. It was slow to prepare. First the leaves were crushed and kneaded into balls. These were dried, broken up, and fermented for three weeks. The smell was disgusting. After a second fermentation, the woad was white and soluble in water. Contact with oxygen in the air made cloth dipped in this white woad turn blue while drying.

Indigo tinctoria was the oriental blue dye that largely replaced woad in the 17th century. It was grown extensively in the American deep south but was ousted by tobacco and cotton, which were more profitable.

The old dyes demanded patience and a wide knowledge of herbs. They could not survive the competition of cheaper, quicker, coal-tar dyes.

◀ *Saffron is still used to dye silk in India and the Far East. It provides the brilliant yellow robes worn by Buddhist monks. Other less costly vegetable dyes have also survived in Asia.*

◆ *Indigo and woad used to be two of the main blue dye plants. Madder and saffron produced red and yellow. The Latin names of most dye plants contain the word* tinctor, *which means 'imparting color.'*

Flower power

The fragrance of flowers was very precious to all those generations who lived before the days of cheap soap and good drainage. Some of the most lyrical passages in the Bible dwell on the pleasures of scent. "Ointment and perfume rejoice the heart," says the proverb, and Solomon's beloved is likened to a garden of "Spikenard and saffron, calamus and cinnamon, with all the trees of frankincense, myrrh and aloes." These spices and gums are still burned in churches to make aromatic smoke.

In the third century B.C., it was etiquette for Chinese officials to sweeten their breath by chewing cloves while talking to the Emperor. Clove oil is one of the flavors in modern toothpastes and forms part of a synthetic carnation perfume. Bad breath has often been considered irreverent; Greek priests would not allow garlic eaters to worship in the temple of Cybele. The hallmark of a Christian saint was to die in an odor of sanctity. Thyme, marjoram, sesame oil and scented gums were often used in embalming.

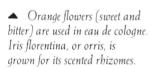

▲ *Orange flowers (sweet and bitter) are used in eau de cologne. Iris florentina, or orris, is grown for its scented rhizomes.*

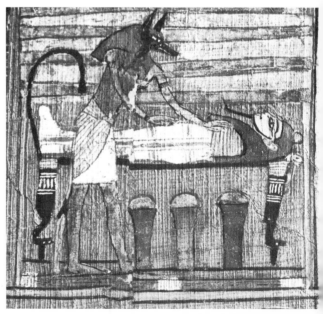

▶ *Anubis, the dog-headed god, embalms the body of the murdered Osiris. In ancient Egypt myrrh, cassia and other aromatics were used to annoint dead bodies.*

The houses of the living were also made to smell pleasant by sweet herbs strewn on the floor. Their scent was released when they were bruised underfoot. More elaborate was the device in Nero's dining room. According to Suetonius, perfume was sprayed onto the guests from pipes hidden behind a ceiling of fretted ivory.

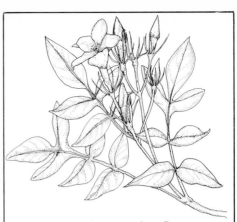

How perfume is made

Most popular perfumes are produced synthetically. Only the most costly lilac and lily-of-the-valley scents are made from real flowers. But lemon verbena, lavender, and the tree *Citrus bergamia* are grown on a large scale for the industry, especially around the Mediterranean.

In the East, patchouli is grown commercially. Steam is used to distill the oil from the leaves. The oil escapes from the still and is cooled by condensers, which separate it from the water. Other leaf oils are distilled in the same way. Flower oils are often extracted by means of a petroleum-based solvent.

Perfumes of Arabia

Muhammad is said to have loved perfume almost as much as the beautiful women who wore it. Among the exotic perfumes created in the Muslim world, is the legendary attar of roses. The petals of 170 damask roses make a single drop of oil. The attar has been distilled in the Bulgarian "Valley of the Roses" for more than 200 years.

Eau de cologne can contain oils of rosemary, bergamot, and cardamom, but orange flowers give it its keynote. Clary sage is sometimes also included. The first bottle of eau de cologne was created by Johann Maria Farina, an Italian who lived in Germany in the 17th century.

Jasmine and some other flower perfumes are produced by the process called *enfleurage.* The petals are spread on glass plates, which have first been smeared with oil. Each day the petals are replaced with a fresh supply until the oil has reached the required level of intensity. The oil is then drained off and bottled. The most expensive scents are composed of these oils.

Enfleurage is used very little by modern perfume manufacturers, but very small quantities of the concentrated oil are added to blends to improve their quality.

Laying out an herb garden

An herb garden is for daily use and needs to be as near the kitchen as possible. Plants do best in conditions that are nearest to those they enjoy in the wild. Most herbs prefer a light, well-drained soil and plenty of sun. It is easier to keep the annuals separate and so avoid treading on the perennials when preparing the bed in spring. Enjoy your herbs when they are young and fresh. Don't wait until they are big and coarse.

▲ *Thyme and marjoram both do well in a rock garden.*

◀ *Rosemary and tarragon are Mediterranean plants and grow in full sun.*

▶ *Plant tall herbs at the back so they don't rob the dwarfs of sunlight.*

▼ *Mint and chives flourish in a quite shady bed.*

A traditional "knot" herb garden

▲ Geometrically arranged knot gardens were once very popular. They are practical, as well as attractive, since most herbs prefer not to be over-shadowed by taller plants. Stepping-stones allow you to reach the center without getting muddy feet or crushing young plants. Experiment with circles, diamonds, triangles, and other traditional shapes.

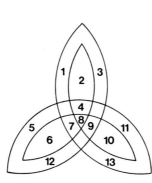

Key
1. *Thyme*
2. *Lemon balm*
3. *Parsley*
4. *Marjoram*
5. *Chervil*
6. *Sage*
7. *Borage*
8. *Rosemary*
9. *Tarragon*
10. *Mint*
11. *Chives*
12. *Dwarf nasturtium*
13. *Rue*

Grow your own herbs

Perennial herbs can be increased by several different methods. Dividing is the simplest. Only do it when the plant is obviously healthy and well-established and at the time of year recommended. This is usually when plants are at their least active. Small plants can be pulled apart by hand. Separate large clumps with a spade. Don't plant the divisions too deeply. Make a hole that is large enough to spread the roots; distribute the soil evenly around them, and press down firmly all around the top of the new plant. Avoid bruising the roots, and be gentle with the stems and leaves of evergreens.

Fennel will grow as high as 1.5 m (5 ft), so it must be given plenty of space. The feathery foliage and yellow flowers are most attractive seen en masse.

Fennel likes soil that holds some moisture, but it also needs plenty of sun. Divide plants after three years to keep them vigorous.

To ensure a regular supply of fresh leaves for salads, keep cropping the shoots almost to the base. Let others flower, and use their seeds in sauces. Fennel is particularly good with fish. The seeds are easy to store, and they retain their delicate anise flavor.

Finocchio, which the English call Florence fennel, is the bulbous stem at the base of the leaf stalk. It is a delicious vegetable, cooked or raw.

Fennel was one of the sacred herbs of the Anglo-Saxons and, in the 16th century, "much used in drinks to make people more lean that are too fat."

Winter Savory is a low, bushy perennial and needs a light soil – not too moist – with plenty of sun. Divide or take cuttings in March. It can also be layered. Savory deserves to be more popular. It has a mass of purplish white flowers and a strong, almost spicy, taste. It dries well and can usefully be added to a homemade tomato soup, to all bean dishes, smoked meats, and fish. It should also be pointed out that it was once regarded as an aphrodisiac.

Dividing

▲ Large clumps benefit from being divided into smaller plants.

Lovage is another giant. It sometimes reaches 2.5m (8 ft), with a handsome spread of dark leaves and pale greenish flowers. It will grow on any soil except heavy clay. Add plenty of compost to the ground before planting. Divide in spring or autumn. Cut the foliage often, but always leave the young leaves at the center. Leaf and seed both have a strong, yeasty flavor particularly good in soups, stews, and stocks. Culpeper prescribed washing in lovage water to remove spots and freckles.

▲ The newly divided herb will soon be the size its parent was. Give it space.

Mints There are many species of this highly flavored herb. Spearmint is grown or mint sauce. Black peppermint makes a better mint tea. All varieties must be grown in a separate bed or have their root space confined. Put into well-manured ground. Gather young leaves as soon as they appear; when they get older, they have less flavor.

Eau de cologne mint is grown for its fruity scent. Some people think the name orange mint is more apt. Like many scented herbs, it needs sun; but like all mints it is a rapid grower. Some of its runners even appear above ground. Pennyroyal is a creeping mint that can be grown to form turf. Plant small pieces at 15 cm (6 in) distances in spring. It will only need trimming twice a year. Pennyroyal does not appear in many modern recipes.

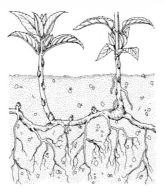

▲ *Mint roots run hungrily just beneath the surface of the soil.*

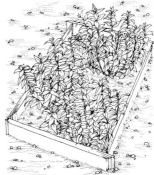

▲ *Bury a frame of brick, slate, or concrete to contain the growth.*

Dividing Chives

Chives are the easiest herbs to grow. Sow seeds in April. Chives grow best where the soil is not too dry. In a sunny location, water them often if the summer is hot. The flowers are cheerful pink tufts, and afterwards the leaves become coarse. So trim the buds off all but a few plants. Let the flowers seed, and next year chives will be all around the garden. The more you cut the leaves, the more they grow.

Use chives in salads, in mashed potatoes, and in cheese dips. In early summer, when onions may be scarce, a generous quantity of chives cooked in oil, will do instead. Culpeper advised against eating them raw, "for they send up very harmful vapors to the brain." This slander is quite unfounded.

Garlic is grown for its strong flavored bulbs, each of which is made up of ten or more sections known as cloves. Plant the cloves 5 cm (2 in) deep and at least 15 cm (6 in) apart in late autumn, preferably in a light soil that gets the sun. But the plants must be watered in mid-summer. By August, the leaves die down and the crop should be dug up. Dry garlic away from the sun in an area that is dry but has good air circulation to prevent rotting. Cloves planted in spring will be ready to harvest in late autumn. Garlic was once known as "the poore man's Treakle"; that is, a remedy for all disease. Pliny said, "the very scent thereof chaseth serpents and scorpions away." People who have not enjoyed the taste of garlic may be chased away by its scent, but it is an essential ingredient in French, Italian, Indian, and Middle Eastern cookery. It must be used with courage.

Thyme Of the various species, common thyme is the most popular, but lemon thyme is also full of flavor. Silver thyme is grown largely for its decorative quality. All like light, well-drained soil and look good in a rock garden. Sunlight brings out the flavor. Thyme often layers itself without the gardener's help. If not, encourage it to do so in spring. Cuttings will also take. Divide well-established plants in autumn. Being an evergreen, the herb must not be cut too heavily in late summer, or it may not survive the winter. Thyme is easily dried. Besides its place in the bouquet garni, it is delicious in cheese sauces, with eggs, or rubbed on most meat before roasting. According to Shakespeare, the queen of the fairies' bed was a bank "whereon wild thyme blows." Sniffing a posy of thyme was Gerard's cure for "paines in the head."

Layering

Wild Marjoram is also known as oregano and is the easiest species to grow. Sweet marjoram has a more subtle flavor but has to be treated as an annual in gardens subject to frost. Oregano needs maximum sun and a very well-drained soil. It also benefits from lime. Each year it sends up 20-cm (8 in) leaf stems, followed by flowers that are pink with a hint of purple. In autumn it dies back. Divide then or in the spring. Take cuttings or sow seeds in spring. If April and May are dry, marjoram will need to be watered. Protect the roots in winter with a light covering of peat or leaf mold. Oregano is used in pizza, onion soup, and all meat dishes. The strong flavor is excellent in homemade sausages and is important in a bouquet garni. The Greeks believed that when marjoram sprouted on a tomb, it was proof that the dead person was happy. This aromatic herb can still be found in perfume and was one of the strewing herbs that sweetened medieval rooms.

Sage is best grown in soil that is not too wet or heavy. It likes the sun. Increase from layers or cuttings made in April. Strong plants can also be divided in autumn or spring. After two or three years sage tends to become straggly, so have young plants ready to replace the old ones. When gathering the herb, never cut back to the wood; new leaf growth is only made from soft stems. Varieties with narrow leaves are easier to dry than are the broad-leaved types. But you can pick a few fresh leaves from time to time in winter. Purple sage is grown for its foliage, which contrasts well with the silvers and dark greens of so many other herbs. In the 16th century, it was said that "sage is used commonly to stuffe veale, porke, and rosting pigges, and that for good cause." Try it also in cheese omelets and herb bread.

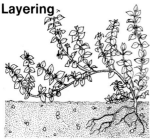

▲ *Layer thyme in April from stems that grow horizontally near the base of the plant.*

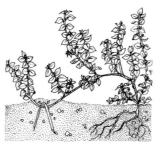

▲ *Pin the stem to the ground with a hoop of bent wire. Submerge in the soil.*

▲ *By June the new roots should be strong enough to transplant. Sever from the old plant.*

Rosemary is an evergreen bush with leaves like pine needles. In spring it has clusters of bright blue flowers. It is grown for its appearance by many people who do not take advantage of the delicious leaves. Tall varieties may reach 2 m (6.5 ft) or more; there are also miniatures suitable for a rock garden. All like sun and a rather dry soil with some lime in it. Rosemary will not survive long periods of frost, so in cold districts, or where the soil is heavy and wet, it is best grown in a planter. Take cuttings in June, filling the pot with a mixture of peat and coarse sand. Keep out of the sun until good strong roots have developed. Use rosemary with eggs, meat, fish, and in sweet jellies. Its perfume was once believed to improve the memory. Rosemary is a great favorite with bees in an herb garden.

Bay. This evergreen becomes a 10 m (33 ft) tree in the perfect climate. But it is happy to be kept clipped back as a decorative shrub. Like rosemary, it is vulnerable to severe frosts. So although it will usually live through the winter, it is safer to grow it in a large tub. In cold weather, it can be moved to a sunny greenhouse or inside the house. In spring, take cuttings of young shoots before they become too woody. There should always be a bay leaf in a bouquet garni and in curries.

Tarragon. Russian tarragon is taller; but the French variety, which is about 1 m (3 ft) tall, has a far better flavor. The roots must be allowed a great deal of space, and the soil must be well-drained. Cold, wet soil often results in tarragon's dying in winter. Sun brings out the flavor. Take cuttings any time up to June. Pull off underground runners in spring, but only if the plant is obviously strong. In places where frosts are severe or long lasting, cover the roots with a layer of leaf mold or straw in autumn. The herb has a stronger flavor if it is cut often and not allowed to become long-legged. Tarragon dies down in winter, but its season can be extended by keeping a potted plant in a sunny sill or in a greenhouse. Cook it with chicken and with marjoram in omelets. It is also the essential ingredient in Béarnaise sauce.

Lemon verbena is a tree that came to Europe from Chile in the 18th century. It is another herb susceptible to hard frosts and suitable for growing in a large pot. But it will do well in a really sheltered warm garden. It likes a dry soil. Take young wood cuttings in early summer. The leaves have a strong lemon scent and flavor and make a very relaxing tea. They can also replace lemon in both sweet and savory dishes.

Taking cuttings

▲ *Pull off a shoot with a "heel."*

▲ *Strip the stem of its leaves for half the length.*

▲ *Insert cuttings around the edge of a well-drained pot.*

▲ *Keep in the shade until new growth appears. Transplant.*

Borage can be sown from March onward if it is to flower. It prefers a well-drained soil but survives heavier conditions, though it needs sun. Keep young plants free of weeds. Self-sown seedlings will always appear after the first year. Dig these up with the soil around their roots and put them where they are wanted, with 50 cm (20 in) of space all around.

Float the blue flowers on the surface of cool summer drinks. The moist cucumber-flavored leaves can be chopped into salads and cheese dips. Culpeper used borage "to expel melancholy."

Basil has to be grown as an annual in cold climates, though it is a perennial in its native India. It hates to be transplanted, so start a few seeds in a 13 cm (5 in) pot. Pinch out all but two of the seedlings and eat the rest in a salad. After the last frost, put the pots out in the sun. You can bury them up to their rims in a bed with other herbs. Pick regularly, and make sure that no flowers form. Bring back indoors in early autumn. Basil is said to discourage house flies, and you will also enjoy an extra month or two of fresh herb. Serve in tomato-based sauces, with poultry, fish, and meat.

Parsley is the one herb that everyone knows. It is strictly a biennial but grows better as an annual. Sow from April onward in a fairly moist soil. Sow very thinly. Germination is often slow. Thin the seedlings to 20 cm (8 in) apart. Sow again in June and August. Keep free of weeds, and water in dry spells. Parsley is also attractive to slugs. Pick often and leave only the green center of the plant. Never allow parsley to flower. The flavor is perfect with most vegetables and in fish dishes. This vitamin-rich herb should be eaten, even when served as a garnish.

Sowing seeds outside

▲ The ground should be well prepared and weed-free before seeds are sown. Break up any surface lumps with a fork.

▲ Sow in a straight line along a string tied to a peg at each end of the row. Sow very thinly, or plants will choke each other.

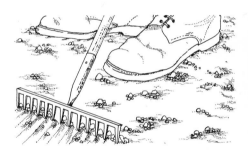

▲ Remove any large stones and then rake to a fine tilth.

▲ Lightly cover the seed with soil by drawing the back of the rake over the surface. Label each herb and the date when sown.

Chervil is one of the *fines herbes* of French cooking. Sow in early spring. The soil must not be too wet. Nor will chervil survive if baked by continuous sun. Thin out so that each plant has 30 cm (12 in) of clear space.

Start picking after about two months. The herb may continue to produce greenery through the winter.

Dried chervil has very little of the delicate flavor of the fresh herb. Use the herb in generous quantities in salads, sauces, and egg dishes. It is also delicious with spinach.

Dill is a yellow umbellifer slightly taller than coriander. Sow in April to ensure a harvest of ripe seeds. Thin to 30 cm. (12 in.) apart. Stake the plants if they are in a windy location. Never grow dill close to fennel, as cross pollination will produce a hybrid of inferior flavor. Cut the flower heads before the petals drop, and hang upside down in bunches in a cool place. Put a large bowl underneath to catch the seeds. Chop the leaves into a potato salad.

Dill seed is an age-old ingredient for baby's colic water. For adults, it is tasty in stews and pickles.

Coriander is one of the few umbelliferous herbs that do not require a large amount of space. Sow in early spring and thin out to 50 cm (20 in) intervals. Coriander likes sun and grows about 1 m (3 ft) tall. Plant it where it will not be overshadowed by other plants. It is grown for the seeds. Collect them as soon as the tiny pale pink flowers have fallen. Store in an airtight tin or jar, in a dark place. They add flavor to curry and other spicy Asiatic food. A teaspoonful of ground seed transforms a hot apple pie. The manna found by Moses in the desert was compared to coriander seed.

Sowing seeds indoors

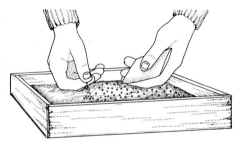

▲ Rather than sow seeds in a cold heavy soil, sprinkle them thinly in a box of moistened seed compost.

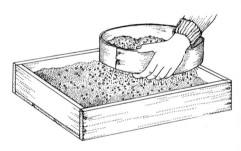

▲ Cover the seeds with a fine layer of compost. Sow one variety per box and label clearly. Water sparingly.

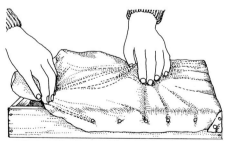

▲ Cover the box with a thick sheet of dark polyethylene or layers of dry newspaper. Seeds germinate faster in the dark.

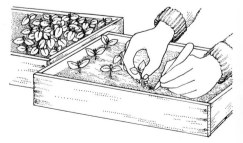

▲ Remove the polyethylene as soon as the young leaves appear. Prick out into another box.

44

1. Basil
2. Thyme
3. Sage
4. Tarragon
5. Mint
6. Marjoram
7. Borage
8. Parsley

Drying and storing herbs

You can enjoy your home-grown herbs all year round by taking a little care in drying them. The aim is to preserve most of the natural color and all the volatile oils that give them their flavor. Cut on a warm, dry day in July as soon as the dew has evaporated but before the sun is really hot. Use a very sharp knife or scissors, and handle the leaves very gently. Be careful not to crush or bruise them. Take no more than a third of the growth on evergreen perennials; annuals will stand more wholesale harvesting. Most annuals and tarragon will produce a second crop in the autumn.

Drying herbs

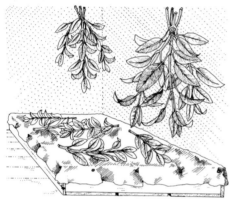

▲ Cover a frame with net. Spread leaves very thinly. Dry in a warm, well-aired place.

▲ Turn the leaves daily to make sure that they dry evenly.

▲ Strip the leaves from the stems as soon as they are crisp. If left too long they become powdery.

▲ Store in airtight jars. Herbs keep better in the dark. Paint the outsides of jars and make labels that show the name and date.

Freezing herbs

▶ Deep freezing is a reliable way of preserving herbs. Pick long stems. Tie in bunches, and knot a strong length of cotton to the end. Dip in boiling water for one minute. Leave the cotton trailing to avoid scalded fingers.

◀ Hang the bunches of herbs on a hook or drain them in a collander. The leaves must be completely dry before they are wrapped for the freezer.

▶ Wrap in clear polyethylene. Before doing so, divide the herbs into the quantities required for a single recipe. A mixture of rosemary, marjoram, chives, and tarragon is good with chicken. Chop the chives before freezing. Make up bouquets garnis.

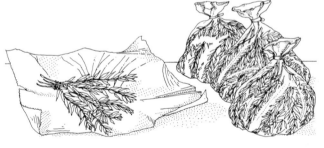

◀ Box the herbs to prevent their being crushed in the freezer. Box single herbs or mixtures for particular recipes together. Label clearly. Only remove herbs from the freezer when they are going to be used at once.

Herbs for beauty

A colorful garden can be created using only those species that were once listed as herbs. Many plants suitable for the herbaceous border come into this category. Goldenrod and valerian were once used for medicine; lavender and lily-of-the-valley, for their scent; and the autumn crocus and Christmas rose contain alkaloids that were used to relieve suffering. The long history attached to these plants is not, of course, the only reason for growing them. Each provides color, form, and texture; and some are richly scented. Silver, variegated, and evergreen foliage help to make a garden enjoyable throughout the year.

A garden should reflect the personal tastes of its owner. And there is enough variety in the long list of old herbal plants to please everyone. Many species now have such big, bright, long-lasting flowers that the old herbalists would hardly recognize them.

The health of plants depends on the condition of the soil. Prepare the permanent border before planting. Heavy clay needs to be dug and exposed to frost. Then add as much peat as you can afford. Enrich light soils with manure.

The seeding of a mixed border is important, as most annuals and many perennials do well only in full sunlight. But if your garden is overshadowed by buildings or trees, be consoled that St.-John's-wort and periwinkle will flourish in a dark corner. Parkinson made a sciatica cure from the seeds of the old English tutsan or "All Heal." Variegated periwinkle boasts bright blue flowers in spring. Gerard said that "the leaves eaten by man and wife together causeth love." Both these plants require little attention and rapidly cover a bank. Take care that they do not suffocate the plants nearby.

Oxford blue and white pansies can be grown from seed under glass in March and planted out in May. Or sow them where they are to flower. Pansies like a moist, rich soil. Pick off the dead heads to ensure a long season.

Viola odorata, a violet, is a tiny bloom with an outsize perfume. The Christmas rose needs protection from slugs. Lilies of the valley are slow to establish themselves, but then need to be restrained or will swamp their neighbors.

Lungwort produces a mass of mauve and blue bells. They make a good foil for dwarf daffodils in spring flower arrangements.

These plants are all happy in the shade and, in hot weather, should be given an occasional watering. Divide them when they become too crowded.

Key to illustration

1. *Sunflowers* 2. *Goldenrod* 3. *Mullein* 4. *Bergamot* 5. *Silver leaf thyme* 6. *Marigolds* 7. *Catmint* 8. *Valerian* 9. *Foxgloves* 10. *Angelica* 11. *Achillea gold plate* 12. *Poppies* 13. *Autumn crocus* 14. *Nicotiana* 15. *Lungwort* 16. *Lily of the valley* 17. *Christmas rose* 18. *Violet* 19. *St.-John's-Wort* 20. *Periwinkle* 21. *Rose* 22. *Pinks* 23. *Pansies* 24. *Lavender* 25. *Chamomile* 26. *Lemon verbena* 27. *Bay* 28. *Acer*

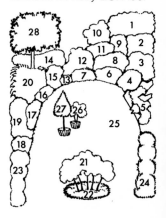

A scented garden

A garden should delight the nose as well as the eye. A chamomile lawn was popular in the Renaissance. It has to be weeded by hand, as chemicals that kill weeds also kill chamomile. Eighty plants are needed per square yard. Sow in boxes and plant at 10 cm (4 in) intervals when 5 cm (2 in) high. The lawn must not be allowed to flower. Set the blades of the lawn mower high when cutting. The reward for all this work is the rich aroma released when chamomile is walked on.

Perfume and color

In the island bed pictured is a richly scented damask rose, Madame Hardy. It has a long flowering season and handsome shape. The pinks encircling it are equally fragrant. There are varieties of *Dianthus alwoodii* in shades from white to deepest red. They can be grown from seeds or cuttings. Always plant them thickly.

Spike lavender sometimes has the species name *Officinalis*. Its silver leaves provide year-long interest. Plant in a light soil and prune into shape in spring.

The spicy smelling catmint dies back in winter. Trim it then and increase by division or from seed. Its cushion of grey foliage and blue flowers make an informal edge to a border.

Vigorous perennials

The magnificence of angelica at its full height of 2.5 m (8 ft) compensates for the four years you wait for flowers. Goldenrod once went into lotions for sores and ulcers. It makes a fine display in late summer. Divide often, and it thrives in shade or sun. For the center of a border, choose the shorter *S. virgaurea*. Valerian owes its name to its healing powers (*Valere* means "to heal"). It flowers most of the summer. Culpeper used it "to draw thorns from the flesh."

Valerian

Catmint

Lavender

Bay

Angelica

Sunflower

Mullein

Achillea gold plate

Nicotiana

Bergamots have a heady scent and unusual flowers in tufts around the stem. Give them a moist soil. Divide, or sow from seed.

Herbalists treat lung conditions with mullein. There are large, flowered perennials, as well as taller biennials. Grow in a rather dry soil. The leaves have a delightful woolly texture.

Oriental poppies do not appeal to the orderly-minded. Support the gleaming scarlet flowers with bush twigs. Save the large seed heads to increase. Among a hundred other lovely medicinal herbs, try tansy, scabiosa, southernwood, and opulent peony.

St.-John's-wort

Effortless annuals

The achillea is a garden version of wild yarrow, the wound-herb, that Achilles was taught to use by Chiron the centaur. Divide every three years. Stake against high winds. There is also a rose-pink variety. Foxgloves may be biennial or perennial. Some very strong colored varieties exist, all with the characteristic deep speckles. They do not mind shade.

Sow sunflowers in April against a wall or fence. Keep them at least 30 cm (12 in) apart. Tobacco flowers fill the evening air in late August with their rich scent. There are many colors. Sow under glass in March, transplant in May. Marigolds sow themselves after the first year.

51

Herbs in pots and window boxes

An herb garden in window boxes or pots can be most enjoyable and convenient, even for people with gardens. Good drainage in the containers and plenty of sun are essential. Herbs that grow bleakly on a dark, north-facing sill will give little joy. In summer all herbs prefer to be outside. If it is impossible to put them on a ledge at least make sure that the window is often open. Scented geraniums live happily inside, and the lemon-scented variety has many uses in the kitchen. Mint, tarragon, basil, and chives, which all die down in the open, will continue to provide fresh herbs for most of the winter in a warm, bright, draft-free kitchen.

Filling a pot

At the bottom, put a layer of broken clay pot or a few irregular-shaped stones. Do not block the drainage hole. Add about 50 mm (2 in) of garden sand, then potting compost. Make a well for the herb and settle compost around the roots. Fill to about 25 mm (1 in) below the rim of the pot. Water thoroughly.

Stand the pot on a saucer or bowl, and always pour away any excess water. Feed your herbs with liquid fertilizer, which is widely available and inexpensive. Follow the manufacturer's instructions.

▲ On a patio or wide balcony, troughs of herbs can be ranged at different heights simply by standing the trough at the back on a row of bricks. Plants grown like this need to be cropped regularly to prevent overcrowding.

▶ Terracotta pots are manufactured in a variety of interesting shapes. These strawberry pots are very suitable for growing parsley. Sow seeds in the top in the ordinary way. Then press one or two seeds into each of the side holes. Growing parsley in these pots helps to keep it free from slugs and other pests. They can be watered from the top or bottom.

▼ Decorative tubs and pots of herbs can make the focal point of a patio. Or group them together on steps. Geraniums or petunias will enliven the effect by adding bright color. Where space is restricted, a whole herb garden can be grown in a pot with wide pockets. Make sure the drainage is very good, and water each pocket separately.

Remember that many herbs prefer dry soil. If a pot like this one stands in a corner, the back pockets should be left empty. Otherwise, rotate the pot every few days to give each herb its share of sunlight.

Herbs on a windowsill

Pots and boxes must be very securely anchored to your windowsill. Mint is tough and may even survive a sudden descent to street level. The head on which it lands may be less hardy. If you grow herbs in pots, a board in front of them, nailed to the wall on either side, looks neat and prevents accidents. Screw angle irons to the surface of the sill to keep window boxes steady.

Thyme, marjoram, sage, and basil all flourish on a window ledge. So does mint, if it is in a separate, large container. In summer, wait until herbs are out of the sun before watering. Then use tepid water. See pages 38-45 for hints on the propagation of all these herbs.

Nasturtiums put color into a window box. They are also highly edible. The leaves are tasty in sandwiches or chopped into cottage cheese. The

pickled seeds can be used like capers.

Chives need less sun than most herbs but are more susceptible to aphids when grown in a pot. Take action at once. Put one squirt of liquid soap into an empty dishwashing liquid bottle. Fill with water. Douse the plant.

Rosemary and bay are happy in pots and can be kept as decorative miniature trees by cooks who crop their leaves often.

Cooking with herbs

There are no firm rules about cooking with herbs and spices. The amount of thyme, sage, or caraway you include in a recipe is a matter of personal taste. But dried herbs have about twice the strength of fresh ones. In most cooking, only a subtle taste is needed. Experiment with a new herb to find out how much you need.

Key

Recipes are for 4 people unless otherwise stated.

To metricate recipes

1 pint = .473 l
1 oz = 28.349 g
1 lb = 0.453 kg

Lentil and rosemary soup

1 lb red lentils
½ lb potatoes
1 qt stock
1 tsp dried rosemary
    (double, if fresh)
piece of lemon skin
salt and pepper

All sorts of dire warnings are issued about the danger of over-seasoning with rosemary. This soup breaks the rules by depending on a definite herb flavor.

Wash the lentils and put them in a pan. Scrub or peel the potatoes and add them, chopped into small cubes. Add the stock and rosemary. Bring to a boil slowly, watching it carefully. Once the foam has subsided, turn the gas very low and simmer for about 30 min. After 20 min. add the lemon peel. This is an extremely thick soup and ideal for cold, wet nights. It can be thinned with additional stock, if necessary.

Red cabbage

1 lb firm red cabbage,
    coarsely chopped
2-3 small onions
1¼ tsp tarragon vinegar
½ large cooking apple,
    chopped
1¼ tsp caraway seed
8 green olives, sliced
3 oz dried fruit
salt and black pepper
oil

Cover the bottom of a thick pan or iron casserole with a little oil. Chop the onions and cook until translucent. Add chopped apple, cabbage, and all other ingredients. Cover tightly. Leave on very low flame for 20-25 min. Stir occasionally. The cabbage should be slightly crisp. It will still be delicious, even if left to cook longer because the guests arrive late.

Marjoram casserole

2 lbs potatoes
¼ lb onions
6 oz cheese
2½ tsp marjoram (more,
    if fresh)
seasoning
14 oz can of tomatoes

Slice the potatoes into very thin discs. Put a layer into a well-greased casserole. On the bed of potatoes sprinkle chopped onions, some of the grated cheese, marjoram, chopped tomatoes, and seasoning. Cover with another layer of potatoes, and repeat, finishing with potatoes. Pour the juice from the tomatoes over the top. This dish tastes good whether baked at 350 F for 1¼ hr. or in a very slow oven (250 F) for 2-3 hr.

Hard boiled eggs stuffed with cottage cheese, chives, and cayenne

To stuff six eggs:
4 oz cottage cheese
A good handful of chives
   (rehydrate dried chives
   in a little water if you
   have no fresh ones)
cayenne
seasoning

Boil the eggs until firm. When cool, peel and cut in half crosswise. Remove the yolks and mash in a bowl with all the other ingredients. Cut a small slice off the base of each egg half. Fill the whites with the mixture and stand the eggs in a bowl. Cover, and put in the bottom of the refrigerator until 5 min. before serving.

Avocados with tarragon mayonnaise

3 avocados
1 large egg yolk
½ c + 2 Tb olive oil
1¼ tsp dry mustard
1¼ tsp lemon juice
2½ tsp dried tarragon
   (more, if fresh)
salt and pepper

In a bowl mix together the mustard, egg yolk, and seasoning. Add the oil, in droplets, stirring with a wooden spoon until the mixture thickens. Once half the oil is used up, you can add it a little faster. Add the tarragon and lemon juice.

Halve the avocados lengthwise and remove the seeds. Scoop out the flesh and cut into small cubes. Pour the sauce over the avocado, pile it back into the skins, and serve on lettuce.

Fish stew with thyme and saffron

2 lbs of boned and fileted
   white fish
½ c + 2 Tb olive oil
1 finely chopped clove
   of garlic
1 Tb chopped onions
1 Tb chopped green pepper
1¼ tsp dried thyme
   (double, if fresh)
pepper and salt
1¼ tsp saffron

Cook the onion, garlic, and green pepper in the oil. Add the fish, cut into chunks, the saffron, and thyme. While very hot, add enough water to cover and cook fast until the fish is edible but still in firm pieces. Serve immediately with chunks of crusty bread to absorb the sauce.

Fish pie

1 lb smoked haddock
1¼ c milk
½ Tb butter
½ Tb flour
2½ tsp fresh chopped
   parsley
1 chopped hard-boiled egg
lemon juice and seasoning
Topping:
1 lb potatoes (cooked
   and mashed)
1¼ tsp sour cream
handful of chopped chives
½ Tb butter

Poach the fish in the milk. Melt the butter over low heat, add the flour, and blend with a wooden spoon. Add the milk slowly, stirring all the time. When it thickens, remove from the heat. Put the fish in the bottom of a well-greased dish, sprinkle with herbs, lemon juice, chopped egg and seasoning. Pour the sauce over all. Mash the sour cream into the potato with the chopped chives. Spread on top of the dish. Dot the surface with the butter. Bake in a moderate oven (375 F) until brown.

Mint sauce

One of the joys of growing your own mint is that you no longer have to pay good money for an overpriced bottle of mint sauce to pour over your lamb. It is very easy to make.

Chop very finely ¼ c + 1 Tb of mint. Add wine or malt vinegar until the cup is within 1 Tb of being full. Stir in 1 tsp sugar. Leave for about 30 minutes to develop its full flavor.

Peanut and thyme rissoles

Even people who dislike the idea of cooked peanuts can eat these rissoles, as it is very unlikely they will be able to identify the ingredients. With the rissoles, serve a salad of grated raw carrots with French dressing and chopped mint.

3 oz peanuts, roasted
   or raw
½ lb onions
5 tsp oil
½ c toasted breadcrumbs
5 tsp dried thyme
   (double, if fresh)
1 2/3 c stock
2 eggs
pepper and flour

Chop the onions finely and cook in the oil. Cover the pan with a lid. When the onions are soft, add the finely ground peanuts, thyme, breadcrumbs, pepper, and stock. Cover and cook for

5-10 min., stirring often. Remove from the heat. Beat the eggs, and stir into the mixture. When cool, make the mixture into twelve rissoles, and flour both sides. Fry for a minimum of 5 minutes in hot fat until crisp and brown.

Fish steaks with fennel

4 whitefish steaks
   (about ½ lb each)
1⅔ c milk
1¼ tsp flour
1¼ tsp fennel seeds
tsp salt and pepper

Warm most of the milk with the fennel seeds. Mix the flour with 2½ tsp milk into a thin paste in a cup. Add to the milk in the pan and stir over low heat until the mixture thickens. Add salt and pepper to taste. Lay the steaks side by side in the bottom of a shallow dish. Pour on the sauce. Dot the top with slivers of butter. Bake in a 325 oven for 20-30 min. Test the fish with a fork: it is ready to eat as soon as it will flake away from the bone.

▶ *Avocados with tarragon mayonnaise, bananas with ginger, and the ingredients for Indian kedgeree.*

Beef goulash

2 lbs stewing beef
2 medium-sized onions
2 cloves of garlic
2½ Tb paprika
2½ c stock
6 lemon verbena leaves
  (or the peel of ½ lemon)
1½ c potatoes, chopped
½ c whipping cream
1¼ tsp flour
1 bay leaf

Cut the meat into cubes and flour them. Cook the chopped onion in the bottom of a large pan in a little oil. Add the chopped garlic, paprika, meat, stock, lemon verbena, and bay leaf. Cook on the lowest heat with a very tight fitting lid. After 40 minutes, add chopped potatoes. Ten minutes later add cream. Stir until the liquid has thickened. This goulash is so filling that a side salad is all the accompaniment it needs.

Curry powder

1¼ tsp ground cumin seeds
1¼ tsp ground turmeric
2½ tsp ground coriander
1¼ tsp ground fenugreek
6 cardamom pods,
  seeds only
1¼ tsp garam masala*
1¼ tsp ground chili
1¼ tsp ground ginger
2½ tsp black
  peppercorns
1¼ tsp mustard seed

You can make curry powder with a mortar and pestle or by putting the seeds in a thick polyethylene bag and crushing them with a rolling pin. An electric coffee grinder will also do the job. Make enough for several curries, and store in an airtight jar.

*Available in specialty food stores.

Lamb curry

2 lb cooked lamb, or other
  leftover meat, cut into
  2-in cubes
¼ lb onions
1 cooking apple
1¼ tsp dark molasses
2 oz sultanas
1 clove garlic
salt
1¼ tsp curry powder
1¼ c stock

Cook the chopped onions and garlic in a little fat. Add the chopped apple and curry powder. Cook for a couple of minutes, stirring. Add all other ingredients and bring almost to the boil. Leave on very low heat for at least an hour, with cover on. Serve with boiled rice, and decorate with grated coconut and slices of cucumber. Lime or mango chutney makes a good accompaniment.

Chicken and garlic

A 6-lb chicken
2 bay leaves
2½ tsp thyme
A handful of finely
  chopped parsley
6 finely chopped sage
  leaves (or 1¼ tsp
  dried sage)
1¼ tsp fennel seeds
50 cloves of garlic
  (about five heads)
½ c olive oil
seasoning

Put the bay leaves, thyme, parsley, and sage in the chicken cavity. Brown it in the oil in a frying pan. Lay the garlic and fennel in the bottom of a heavy casserole with a tight cover. Lay the chicken on its bed of garlic. Rub salt and pepper on the skin. Cover, and bake at 350 F for 1½ hr., or until tender. The garlic should be eaten with the bird.

Buttered apples with spices

1½ lbs crisp eating apples
5 tsp soft brown sugar
1 Tb butter
½ tsp ground ginger
½ tsp cinnamon
1 tsp grated nutmeg
4 cloves

Melt the butter over low heat. Add the apples, spices, and sugar. Cover and cook for 20-25 minutes. Stir occasionally to make sure all the apples are coated in sugar and butter. The apples should be cooked, but not mushy. Remove the cloves before serving. This dish is equally good cold.

Rice pudding with lemon geranium

¼ c long-grain rice
2 c milk
3 tsp. sugar
1¼ tsp honey
2 egg yolks, beaten
2 lemon geranium leaves

Wash the rice and put it in a baking dish. Heat the milk slowly and melt the honey and sugar. When they have dissolved, pour over the rice. Gradually add the beaten egg. Add the two leaves. Bake for 2 hr. at 300 F. Remove the leaves before serving. A bay leaf can be used in place of the geranium leaves. A tablespoon of dried fruit can also be added.

Bananas with ginger

4 bananas
½ lemon
1¼ tsp finely chopped ginger
4 oz dark chocolate
2½ tsp white sugar
½ c whipping cream (optional)

Slice the bananas into the bottom of a serving dish. Squeeze the lemon, and pour the juice over the bananas. Mix in the ginger. Cover with the sugar. Grate the chocolate, and cover the other ingredients with an even layer so that only the chocolate shows. Leave in the refrigerator for at least two hours or overnight. Remove from the refrigerator 30 minutes before serving. To make the pudding more spectacular, decorate with whipped cream and candied angelica shortly before serving.

Walnut and parsley soufflé

½ lb chopped onions
3 c + 1 Tb milk
6 Tb butter
5 Tb flour
salt and pepper
5 eggs, separated
4 oz chopped walnuts (half very fine, half still big enough to crunch)
5 tsp chopped fresh parsley

Cook the onions in a little milk. In a separate pan, melt the butter. Add the flour and blend. Very slowly add the remainder of the milk, stirring all the time. When it thickens, remove from the heat. Beat the egg yolks. Add to the sauce when it has become tepid. Pour the onions, milk, and sauce, nuts and parsley into a souffle dish. (Any oven-proof dish will do, provided it is reasonably deep). Beat the egg white until very stiff and fold as quickly as possible into the rest of the mixture. Bake in an oven that has been preheated to 400° for about 40 min. The diners should be waiting at the table with forks raised.

Indian kedgeree, or spiced rice

6 Tb onion
oil
8 peppercorns
8 allspice berries
4 pods of cardamom
6 whole cloves
2 shredded bay leaves
2 tsp chopped fresh ginger
5 oz patna rice, or other
    long-grained rice
4 oz green lentils
3¾ c cold water
salt
2½ tsp mango chutney or
    any other chutney with
    a tang

Pound the spices in a mortar and pestle. If you do not have one, put them into a polyethylene bag and crush them with a rolling pin. Wash and drain the rice and lentils. Cook the onion in a large pan with a little oil. Add the crushed spices and the shredded bay leaves. Add the other ingredients, except the chutney. Bring to a boil, cover tightly, and turn the heat down very low. Cook for 30 minutes. Lift the lid quickly every 5 minutes and stir to prevent sticking. Put the lid on before too much steam escapes. Finally, add the chutney and allow to cook for a few more minutes. By now, all the moisture should have been absorbed; the rice should be well cooked and the lentils should still have some bite. A heaping teaspoon of ground ginger can replace the fresh ginger. Garnish with chopped watercress or serve with sliced bananas and cucumbers.

Tomato and basil salad

Many writers on the use of herbs in cooking seem half apologetic for basil's crisp and slightly acid flavor. Like many a stranger, basil is best met head-on. You must have the fresh green leaves for this salad. If you can only obtain dried herbs, use reconstituted chives instead.

1 lb firm tomatoes
    (preferably beefsteak)
About 30 basil leaves
2½ tsp salad oil
2½ tsp lemon juice
salt and pepper
1 clove garlic

Slice the tomatoes thinly. Layer them in a dish that has been rubbed with a clove of garlic. Tear or shred the basil. (It is said that basil

should never be cut with a knife.) Distribute the herb evenly among the tomatoes. Dress with oil, lemon juice, salt and pepper. Serve the salad on its own or with cold meat or an omelet. Do not waste its flavor by eating it with a highly seasoned dish.

▶ *Lentil and rosemary soup, chicken with garlic, and a tomato and basil salad.*

Herbal oils and drinks

Many delicious hot and cold drinks can be prepared by treating the leaves of herbs as if they were tea. The exact quantities are a matter of taste. As a rough guide, try one teaspoonful of dried herb for every cup. Steep for about five minutes. Pick only the best young leaves if you are planning to use them fresh. Wash, drain, and chop well, just before making the tea. Herbs can also add extra flavor to salad oil and wine vinegar. The first time follow the recipe. Next time vary the quantity of herb, or mix it with others to suit your own palate.

How to make dandelion coffee

Arab aphrodisiacs

Mint tea is particularly refreshing and has been enjoyed in the Middle East for centuries. In hot weather, make a strong infusion. Fill half a jug with fresh mint. Fill with boiling water. Dissolve into this two teaspoons of sugar per person. Strain after ten minutes and leave in the refrigerator until really cool. Serve in glasses with ice cubes, and float borage flowers on the surface. Peppermint makes the nicest tea, but any mint is palatable.

Lemon balm is best drunk hot. It is very relaxing just before going to bed. Balm does not dry well, so make the most of it in summer when it is growing vigorously. An Arab proverb says it makes the heart merry and joyful. Like mint, it was believed to be an aphrodisiac. It is also used in perfume.

Another good sedative tea is lemon verbena. Fresh or dried leaves are equally good. Sweeten with honey, which brings out the flavor beautifully.

▲ Dandelion coffee is tasty and caffeine-free. Dig up large plants and chop off the roots.

▲ Keep the leaves for salad. Scrub the roots and cut up small. Spread on a clean baking sheet.

▲ Put into a preheated oven (375° F). Roast for about an hour. The pieces should be crisp and brown when they are ready.

▲ Grind by hand or in an electric grinder. Put 3 Tb of the coffee into a warm jug. Pour on 2½ c of boiling water.

▼ Put a few sprigs of tarragon, thyme, or oregano into a bottle of oil or vinegar. Leave on a sunny shelf for about two weeks, shaking daily. Then strain the oil or vinegar off into another bottle. Use in salad dressings and for cooking.

▲ A gargle for a sore throat. Steep five teaspoonfuls of chopped red sage in 2½ c of boiling water. Strain after five minutes, and dissolve five teaspoonfuls of honey into the tea. Use night and morning.

Medicinal teas

The teas listed so far are good enough to drink for their flavor alone. It hardly matters whether or not you believe the claims made for them by the old herbalists.

Chamomile tea, made from the flowers, is a gentle way to ease an upset stomach. It also has a beneficial effect on the complexion.

Betony tea, made from the leaves, will sometimes cure a headache. A hot or cold tea, made from the flowers and leaves of bergamot, has a settling effect on the stomach.

63

Wild herbs and their uses

Most of the common weeds that cause gardeners such anguish and backache were once thought of as palatable foods or valuable medicines. Dandelion, stinging nettles, and chickweed all have their uses. If you have no garden, or your garden is a weed-free paradise, gather them in the country. Take care not to pick them in places that have been polluted. Avoid areas that have been sprayed with insecticides or chemical weed killers. Be careful not to kill plants by stripping them of all their leaves.

1

3

1. Ground elder prefers shade; flowers in summer. Eat cooked. An invasive weed in gardens.

2. Red nettle can flower all year. It is tasty as a cooked vegetable and grows in cultivated ground.

3. Good King Henry (English mercury, wild spinach) is related to fat hen but the flower spikes are leafless. It appears from May to August.

4. Chickweed flowers all year round in exposed places and gardens. It is tasty raw or cooked. An infusion can be made to bathe tired eyes.

2

4

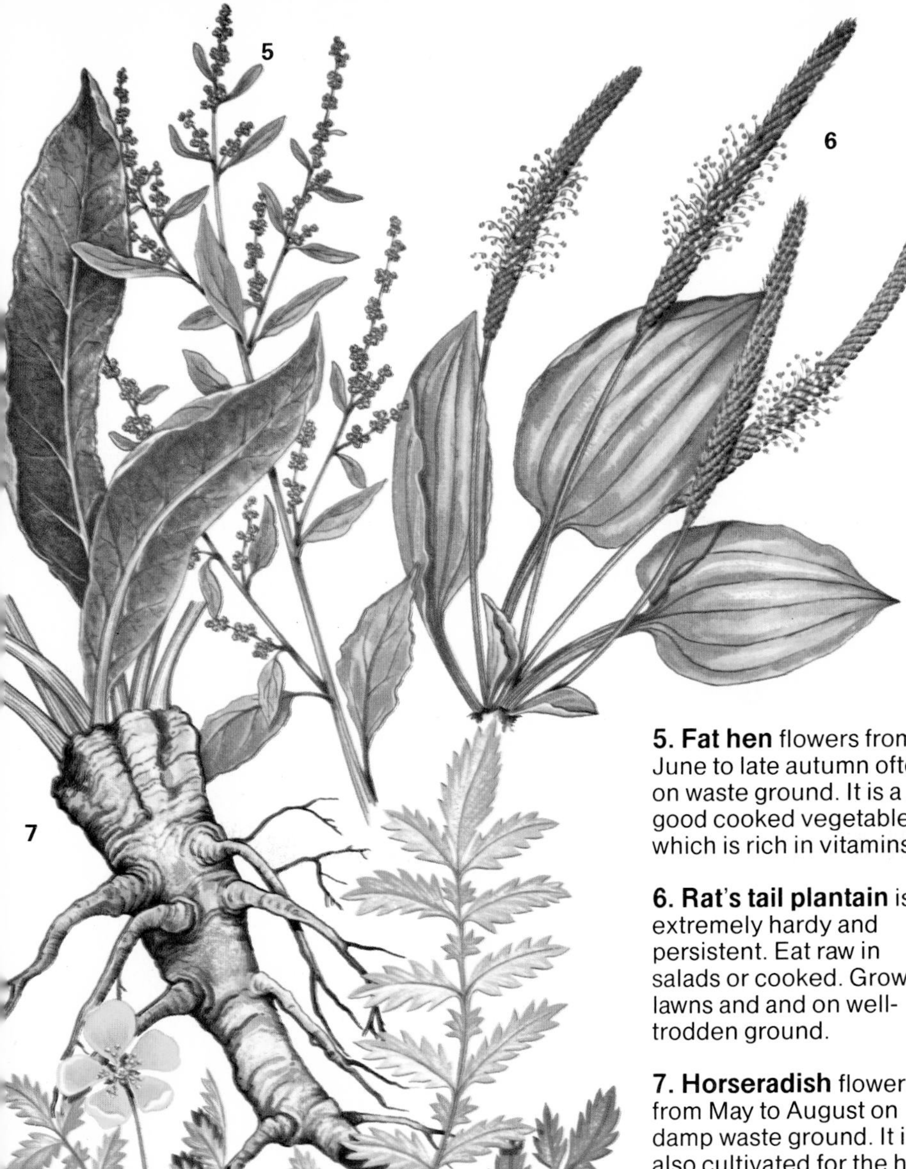

5. Fat hen flowers from
June to late autumn often
on waste ground. It is a
good cooked vegetable,
which is rich in vitamins.

6. Rat's tail plantain is
extremely hardy and
persistent. Eat raw in
salads or cooked. Grows in
lawns and and on well-
trodden ground.

7. Horseradish flowers
from May to August on
damp waste ground. It is
also cultivated for the hot
flavor of its root.

8. Silverweed flowers
from May onward in damp
places. The roots were
widely eaten before the
introduction of potatoes.

Cooking with wild herbs

What could be more satisfying than to make a meal of your weeds? Especially as you did not pay for the seed or have the effort of planting them. A recipe for dandelion coffee is on page 62. The young leaves are good in a salad. Mix them with shredded white cabbage or Boston lettuce, which contrast well with the dark green of dandelion. They also contain lavish amounts of Vitamin C.

Feed the plants, and they will grow to the size of cultivated vegetables. Seed merchants now sell enlarged varieties, which are blanched like chicory.

Weed meals

The stinging nettle is a common pest. Don't curse it, eat it. Serve it cooked or turn it into beer and wine. Culpeper said that a brew of the seeds "is a remedy against the bites of mad dogs." This is not true, but nettles are full of vitamins and minerals. If you refuse to eat them, at least chop them onto your compost heap and give your soil the benefit of all that nitrogen. Many other plants can be cooked in the same way as the stinging nettle. Red nettle is tasty cooked and so are rat's tail plantain and ground elder. The Romans are known to have eaten a lot of ground elder.

Legionnaires were also responsible for the spread of silverweed, which they stuffed in their boots to ease tired feet. It has a tasty root, rather like parsnip, but it is rare to find enough large roots to make a whole meal. Chickweed can be cooked but is even more delicious raw in peanut butter sandwiches. Fat hen and Good King Henry were once both popular vegetables. Fat hen was the *melde,* beloved of the Anglo-Saxons. It was ousted by the arrival of spinach from Asia in the 16th century. Cook like nettles, or make into soup with potatoes, parsley, and milk.

How to cook nettles

▲ Wear gloves to pick nettles. Gather huge amounts of the young yellow-green leaves. Avoid the stalks and old, dark green foliage.

▲ Wash leaves thoroughly and drain in a collander for five minutes. Put into a heavy pan and cover with a tight-fitting lid.

▲ Cook over low heat for 10-15 minutes. Strain off the liquid and keep for stock. Stir in grated nutmeg, butter, salt, and pepper.

Mustard belongs to the same family as the cabbage and radish. White mustard grows mostly in chalky soil. It can be eaten as a salad, either alone or with cress. The flowers start to appear in May and continue well into autumn.

The seeds are used in commercial mustard powder, together with black mustard and turmeric. It is the turmeric that gives it the strong yellow color. Wheat flour and other spices are included to improve the texture and flavor.

Black mustard often grows on cliff tops; it also appears in other damp waste areas and along rivers. The oblong seeds begin to ripen in August.

It takes a good deal of patience to gather enough seeds to make a worthwhile quantity of mixed mustard. But a few of the tasty seeds can be crushed and added to a cheese sauce, or they can be rubbed over poultry and meat before roasting.

The flavor of wild mustard seeds is not overpoweringly hot, but it is deliciously nutty. Curries and other spiced oriental foods benefit from the addition of mustard seed, and it puts a special tang into salad dressings and homemade chutneys.

Season with wild herbs

Wild herbs tend to have a less strong flavor than strains that have been bred selectively for thousands of years. Otherwise treat them exactly like cultivated herbs. Dry them by the process described on page 46. Several of the most useful herbs are umbellifers. Before gathering them in the wild take note of the warning on page 24.

Wild chervil (otherwise known as cow parsley) is much shorter than hemlock. If you are sure it is wild chervil chop the leaves into salads and egg dishes.

Cut a hot baked potato lengthwise. Scoop out the pulp and mash in a bowl with cream, salt, pepper, chervil, and a raw egg. Refill the skins and bake for another 10-15 minutes in a hot oven.

The leaves and seeds of fennel, another umbellifer, give off a scent of aniseed when roughly handled. Make a salad of diced cucumber and slices of crisp eating apple. Dress with oil, lemon juice, chopped fennel leaves, and seasoning.

Sweet cicely has a delicate flavor, and its forest of white flowers is worth having in the garden. It is rarely found in the wild. Gerard ate the leaves in salads and the roots cooked. Follow both good examples. Stew rhubarb, gooseberries, or plums with sweet cicely; only half the usual amount of sugar is needed.

Horseradish

Horseradish can, of course, be grown very easily in a garden. In a small garden it grows almost too easily, except for those who are addicted to the sauce made from its rampaging roots. If you are a lover of this fiery accompaniment to roast beef, you can save money by making your own.

Horseradish is common in waste areas. Dig up a root and scrub it thoroughly. To two tablespoons of the grated root, add 1¼ cups of milk, and 3¾ tablespoons of bread crumbs. Cook slowly for 20 minutes. Add 2½ teaspoons of butter and salt and pepper to taste. Serve cold with sliced meat. Vary this recipe with a little mustard and 3¾ teaspoons of vinegar.

Potpourri and pomanders

A potpourri bowl in your living room will remind you of the scent of your favorite summer flowers, even in midwinter. Or a simple pomander can be made from cloves and an orange. It will last for years, filling a wardrobe or linen closet with a subtle, but not overpowering, perfume. Extra strength is added by rolling the pomander in powdered orris root or gum benzoin. Both are traditional fixatives for flower scents. Make orris at home from the rhizomes of the white iris. Unearth them in summer, peel off the outer husks, and leave to dry in the sun. Ready ground, orris is sold by herbalists and some pharmacies.

How to make a clove orange pomander

▼ *Press cloves into an orange, leaving bare strips on the skin for ribbons. Tie the ribbons tightly, as the orange will shrink as it dries.*

Moth protection

Make a muslin envelope 75 mm (3 in) square and fill with dried lavender, balm, and southernwood. A loop at one corner can be slipped over the hook of a clothes hanger. These herbs will deter moths. Cover the sachets with fabric remnants and give them as small gifts. Use any potpourri mixture.

Thyme, oregano, and rosemary add a warm note to the scent. The dried peel of lemon and orange are also useful. Scented pillows for chairs can be made in the same way.

Herbal pillows

A small scented pillow can make sitting in a comfortable chair seem doubly refreshing. Fill a muslin pillowcase with any potpourri mixture. Make a loose cover of heavier fabric to go on the outside. Attach a lavender-filled pillow to the back of a wing chair with pins, or put it with other pillows on a sofa or divan. Lemon balm, rosemary, and eau de cologne mint are all very agreeable scents for this purpose.

Potpourri ingredients

2 c dried petals and leaves
2½ tsp orris
1¼ tsp gum benzoin
1¼ tsp powdered cloves
1¼ tsp powdered allspice
½ nutmeg (grated)
A few drops oil of rosemary, heliotrope, or other scent.

A potpourri can use any scented leaf, flower, or root that is available. Violets, pinks, and lavender all flower at different seasons. Begin by collecting wide-mouthed jars with tight-fitting lids. Pick your ingredients in dry weather and follow the instructions for drying herbs (page 46). When the petals are dry, store each variety in a separate jar.

Make your mixture when you have gathered enough different petals. Stir them together in a large bowl with orris, benzoin, and spices. Add a few drops of concentrated herb oil for extra strength. Rose geranium and patchouli oils are sold by herbalists and at some pharmacies. Return the mixture to a large jar. Shake daily for two months. Pour out into bowls or boxes.

Herbal cosmetics

Many cheap and effective beauty preparations can be made from homegrown herbs. The basis of most of them is an infusion. Put the herbs in a jug or teapot and steep in boiling water for ten minutes or more. Then strain. Two or three fresh lovage leaves makes a very cleansing bath. Chop the leaves and infuse them in 1 pint of boiling water. Add the strained liquid to your bath. It contains a natural deodorant. Never add herbs directly to bath water: it is very irritating to have to pick off the dozens of leaf particles that stick to the skin.

Bath mixtures

There is no limit to the variety of herbal scents you can enjoy in the bath. A mixture of thyme, lemon balm, lemon verbena, and rosemary is very relaxing and slightly astringent.

A teaspoonful of each of these herbs, dried and crushed, will turn the water a delicate light green. If fresh herbs are used, a larger quantity is needed to produce the same scent. Lavender flowers, bay leaves, hyssop, and marjoram are among the many culinary herbs

worth trying.

A gleaming head of hair

When so many expensive shampoos are on the market all boasting of the herbs they contain, it makes sense to try a home-brewed hair conditioner.

Experiment to see which suits your hair. Those with dark hair should use rosemary or sage. Rosemary develops the highlights; sage tends to deepen the natural shade.

Infuse a tablespoon of either herb in a pint of boiling water. Wash the hair first with your normal shampoo. Rinse thoroughly. Use the herbal conditioner for the final rinse.

For blond hair choose chamomile. Steep half a cup of dried flowers in one quart of boiling water. Leave to cool. Wash the hair. Rinse several times with herbal infusion. Leave on hair for ten minutes. Finally rinse with clear water.

Nettle leaves are said to stimulate hair growth. Follow these same instructions for making the infusion.

Herbal bath infusions

▲ *Give yourself a cleansing and relaxing bath with scented herbs. Put the dried herbs in a square of muslin.*

▲ *Fold together and make a bag by tying a ribbon or a strip of muslin around the bunched up corners.*

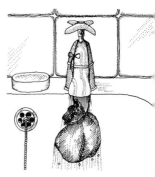

▲ *Suspend the herb bag from the hot-water faucet so that the water flows through it. The bag can be rinsed and reused.*

Ivy oil

▲ A liniment for stiff muscles. Heat a quart of vegetable oil to 104° F.

▲ Put the oil and 3 tsp chopped ivy leaves in a jar in a warm place. Shake daily.

▲ Strain off the oil after two weeks. Rub the liniment into the muscles after a hot bath.

Head to toe

There are many traditional facial treatments based on herbs. Daily washing in elder-flower water is claimed to remove freckles and wrinkles. It will certainly soften the skin. Sage is another effective cleansing lotion. But really oily skins will benefit from being washed in yarrow water. *Achillea millefolium* is the plant needed. Gather it wild, or buy it dried from a herbalist. Make a strong infusion. It is a good remedy for black-heads, and it leaves the skin feeling wonderfully fresh.

For a simple facial, use 2½ tablespoons of fennel seeds. Put them in a cup and add enough boiling water to cover. Leave ten minutes. Beat 3¾ tablespoons of clear honey into a carton of plain yoghurt. Strain the fennel water into the yoghurt and stir. Apply to the face, keeping it out of your eyes. Move your facial muscles as little as possible for the twenty minutes the pack is on. Rinse.

A bath for tired feet

Soak your feet in a bath of nettle water. Use the dried herb, as gathering it fresh is guaranteed to tire your feet further. Steep a cupful of nettles in a jar of hot water. After ten minutes, strain into a large bowl or foot bath. Add enough hot water to reach the ankles. Sit on a comfortable chair and soak for up to ten minutes. Mari-gold leaves are another cure for tired feet.

Herbal cold cream

▲ Pound the herb well. Marjoram, sage, or lemon verbena is very suitable.

▲ Pack the crushed leaves into a wide-mouthed jar. Steep in vegetable oil for about three weeks. Strain, and add fresh herbs until the oil has a strong scent.

▲ Strain the oil and add a few drops to an unscented cold cream. Blend thoroughly.

A-Z of herbs

The following list of herbs covers the common species that can be found wild or cultivated, and also some of the more exotic herbs, usually only found in shops.

A brief description and the major uses, past and present, are given. Medicinal claims for herbs tend to be extravagant and particularly lengthy; in fact, with some herbs one might suppose that a cure for all ills had been found. An attempt has therefore been made to indicate the major medicinal claims of the past and some modern uses, where these are medically acceptable. Where an herb is in any way dangerous, the fact is noted. This list can only be a short selection from the enormous number of plants with herbal qualities. Further reading will reveal many other plants with intriguing claims.

Absinthe see Wormwood

Adder's Tongue *(Ophio glossum vulgatum)* 15-30 cm (6-12 in). A fern. Has one leaf that opens out and produces a dented flower stalk, yellowish-green color, just like an adder's tongue. Grows in damp places in early spring; found in April or May; wilts in heat. Bulb and leaf used medicinally as a poultice for skin problems and internally to induce vomiting.

Adderwort see Bistort

Agrimony *(Agrimonia*

eupatoria) (Liverwort, Stickwort) 30-40 cm (12-16 in). Yellow star-shaped flowers, smelling like apricots, on a spiky stem; long indented leaves, green at top grayish underneath,

Agrimony

covered with little hairs and growing directly from the stem. Found in hedgerows and rough grassland. Medicinally once used as tea made from flowers, as a gargle for mouth inflammations, and sometimes recommended for gall bladder problems.

Allspice *(Pimenta officinalis)* 6-12 m (20-40 ft) Tree. Small white flowers in clusters; leathery oblong leaves. Central and South America. Fruit fleshy, sweet berry, purplish-black when ripe. Berry, dried and ground, used medicinally as a laxative and stimulant. Aromatic.

Almond *(Prunus amygdalus)* 3-6 m (10-20 ft) Tree growing in Mediterranean countries and southern California. Finely serrated leaves on thorny branches; large rose and whitish flowers. Culinary use as common nut and as butter alternative to peanut butter. Bitter oil once used as cough remedy and as external soothing agent.

Cosmetic use of ground kernels and oil as cleansing cream.

Alpine Gentian *(Gentiana lutea)* 100-125 cm (3-4 ft). Large, bright yellow flowers (after root is about ten years old); bright green leaves up to 30 cm (12 in) long and 15 cm (6 in) wide; simple erect stem; thick crinkled root. Found in mountainous areas of south and central Europe and west Turkey. Roots used medicinally for lack of appetite and digestion problems.

Used in food industry for bitter beverages.

Aloe *(Aloe vera)* 1-1½ m (3-5 ft). Yellow to purplish drooping flowers; long narrow whitish-green leaves with spiny teeth; strong fibrous root. Found in east and south Africa and West Indies.

Medicinal use of leaves as powder or juice. "Aloes" is dried juice used as purgative.

Anemone *(Anemone nemorosa)* (Wood anemone) 30 cm (12 in). White, red, or blue flowers; deeply cut leaves on hairy stem; tuberous root. Whole plant once used for healing wounds, but could be irritating and cause depression.

Angelica *(Angelica archangelica)* 1-2 m (3-6.5 ft). Greenish-white flowers in large terminal compound umbels — honey-like odor; leaves grow from dilated sheaths that surround stem, which is round, grooved, hollow and branched near top. Found in damp meadows and along river banks. Flowers June to August. Medicinal use of roots and seeds for digestive problems and as tea to stimulate appetite.

Culinary use of raw roots with butter and young stems as celery; also in confectionary.

Anise *(Pimpinella anisum)* (Aniseed) 30-45 cm (12-18 in). Small white flowers in compound umbels; heart-shaped leaves; round, grooved, branched stem. Flowers July and August; fruit ripens by September. Found wild, but can be grown from seed.

Oil from seeds as drug to stimulate gland secretion and for many other uses.

Whole plant has fragrant odor oil; used as aromatic.

Arnica *(Arnica montana)* (Leopards Bane) 30-70 cm (12-28 in). Yellow daisy-like flower heads June-August, petals notched at outer tips; slightly hairy, lightly branched stem; horizontal dark brown root. Found in mountain areas of Europe.

Used once in the promotion of healing and sometimes as a cardiac agent.

Dangerous.

Arrowroot *(Maranta arundinacea)* 2 m (6 ft). White flowers; leaves with long narrow sheaths and large spreading blades; slender, many-branched stem; creeping root, giving off fleshy tubers. Found in tropics, particularly West Indies and Guiana.

Cultivated largely for the high quantity of edible starch found in the fleshy tubers. Medicinal use of starch today in preparations to calm the stomach and reduce vomiting.

Autumn Crocus *(Colchicum autumnale)* 20-50 cm (8-20 in) Lilac or purple crocus-like flowers in autumn, followed by

smooth, narrow, dark green leaves from base.

Grows from large, dark brown bulb. Found in damp meadows. Medicinal use to relieve gout pain, but is extremely poisonous; contains colchicine.

Used in experiments in the treatment of cancer.

Dangerous.

Avens *(Geum urbanum)* 30-60 cm (12-24 in). Bright yellow, star-shaped drooping flowers June-August; leaves in serrated lobes; erect hairy stem, red at bottom. Found in hedgerows and in deciduous forests in temperate regions.

Medicinally once used as a gargle for gum problems and halitosis.

Balm *(Melissa officinalis)* (Lemon Balm). Up to 1 m (3 ft). Small, pale yellow flowers in clusters; can also be rose or blue-white. Leaves bluntly

Balm

serrated and somewhat hairy, and square. Easy to grow in temperate climate. Sow March-April to plant out in autumn for harvest in the following year.

Culinary use as a substitute lemon flavor. Use chopped leaves. Used in making chartreuse.

Medicinal uses of leaves for soothing and digestive disorders.

Barberry *(Berberis vulgaris)* 1-2.5 m (3-8 ft). Small yellow flowers April-June hanging from branches in clusters. Bright red oblong berries; stems reddish when young but dirty gray when older; root yellow; bark bitter.

Root bark once used for liver ailments; fresh juice of ripe fruit claimed to be good for gums when applied directly.

Basil *(Ocimum basilicum)* 1 m (3 ft). Flowers whitish in whorls on small, light-green leaves clustered around square stem. Larger leaves grayish-green beneath, soft and cool to touch. Can be grown outdoors in temperate climate, but inclined to be delicate as comes originally from India. Culinary use of leaves, being particularly aromatic; increases in flavor when cooked. Peppery flavor when mixed with parsley and savory.

Medicinally once used for digestive disorders and externally in healing compresses and baths.

Bay *(Laurus nobilis)*. Up to 10 m (3 ft). Shrub-like tree often unrecognized. Evergreen, leaves elliptical, tapering to points; undersides pale yellowish green. Can be grown outside (frost will damage or kill) or in tubs indoors.

Culinary use in traditional bouquet garni and often used with fish and vegetables in soups, etc.

Medicinal use of leaves to stimulate appetite.

Belladonna *(Atropa belladonna)*. Up to 1.5 m (5 ft). Single bell-shaped flowers, dull brown to dark purple. Erect leafy stem often splitting into three branches; thick, creeping, whitish fleshy root. Fruit, black shiny berry, size of a cherry. Found in pastures and waste areas.

Medicinal use only by medical direction; narcotic action can produce paralysis and death. Dangerous.

Bergamot Red *(Monarda didyma)* 50-100 cm (20-40 in). Red, crimson, and purple flowers July-September in whorls at top of square stem with oval serrated leaves. Can be grown in rich, moist soil, propagated by division. Flowers and leaves once used as sleep-inducing drink.

Betel *(Areca catechu)*. Palm tree, which is native of Sri Lanka and Malaya and is cultivated in other parts of the tropics. Chewing of the nut, the fruit of the tree, produces mild stimulation. It is estimated that more than 200 million people are addicted.

Betony *(Stachys officinalis)* 15-70 cm (6-28 in). Whorls of red-purple flowers June-August; has leaves on opposite sides of square, hairy unbranched stem. Found in old gardens, meadows, and along forest paths. Plant juice was used to heal cuts, and for asthma and bronchitis.

Bird's Foot Trefoil *(Lotus corniculatus)*. Ground level growth with spreading branches and lots of rings of small leaves. Flowers bright yellow to brownish-red at ends of branches. Found almost anywhere on open ground. Leaves once used to treat nervous pain.

Bistort *(Polygonum bistorta)* (Adderwort). Up to 1 m (3 ft).

Red to rose flowers in spike-like formation; bluish-green leaves at base and a few high tapering leaves on long narrow stem; root is thick, knobbled and twisted into "S" shape. Found in damp mountain areas.

Decoction of root once used for diarrhea; also for infections of the mouth.

Blackberry *(Rubus fruticosus)*. Familiar rambler with white flowers and hairy leaves. Found in hedgerows, etc.

Historically, leaves chewed to stop bleeding gums; also used for diarrhea.

Blackthorne *(Prunus spinosa)* (Sloe) 3 m-4 m (10-13 ft). Tree or shrub, often cultivated for ornamental purposes. Small white flowers grow profusely March-April; small leaves and very thorny branches. Found in hedgerows and on the edge of woods.

Blackthorne

Medicinal use of tea from flowers as a harmless laxative; also stimulates appetite.

Culinary use of fruit in jam makes good laxative for children.

Borage *(Borago officinalis)*. Up to 70 cm (28 in). Blue or purplish star-shaped flowers; leaves grayish-green, bristly, oval, or oblong; hollow, bristly, bunched stem. Grown from seed in March-April, well-drained sunny position. Grows freely.

Culinary use of leaves on bread and butter and sometimes used like spinach; improves cabbage cooking; gives coolness to beverages.

Medicinal use once as a stimulant and against depression; also generally as a refreshing coolant.

Bryony *(Bryonia alba)* (White Bryony) 3 m (10 ft). Small, greenish-white or yellowish flowers June-August; prickly stem with spinal tendrils used for climbing; root dirty white, fleshy, containing milky juice. Can be cultivated in moist soils, but also found in wild. Roots once used as a strong laxative but is very poisonous, as are the berries. Dangerous.

Bugle *(Ajuga reptans)* 30-60 cm (12-24 in). Crowded spikes of blue flowers in May-June; upper leaves growing straight from stem often tinged blue; lower leaves stalked; hairy stems. Found particularly in damp woods and meadows. Leaves have been used as an astringent: bitter taste can be sweetened with honey. Used as sedative for upset stomachs.

Bugloss *(Echium vulgare)* (Viper's Bugloss) 1 m (3 ft). Red and blue flowers June-August; leaves narrow and rough, with stiff hairs, as is the whole plant; stem unbranched.

Found on roadsides, near the sea, and in dry pastures.

Whole plant once used medicinally as a diuretic and expectorant.

Burdock *(Arctium lappa)* 1-1.25 m (3-4 ft). Purple flowers in loose clusters; heart-shaped leaves, smaller higher up; reddish, pithy stem. Familiar seed pods that cling to clothing. Common in hedgerows and waste areas.

Leaves were used to stimulate secretion of bile and to help acne.

Burnet *(Sanguisorba minor)* (Salad Burnet). Flowers gathered into a purplish head with no petals; coarse-toothed leaflets in pairs on slender stems; stout root. Common in grassy places on chalk.

Culinary use of leaves in salads, have a nutty cucumber taste; use as parsley. Best to use homegrown leaves.

Butcher's Broom *(Ruscus aculeatus)* 1 m (3 ft). A low shrub; tiny greenish-white flowers grow singly from center of leaves, which are green, rigid, and end in sharp spikes; branched stems. Round, bright red berries are two or three times as large as holly berries.

Decoction made from twigs once used to promote perspiration and other body water loss.

Butterbur *(Petastites vulgaris)*. Stalk appears in January about 30 cm (1 ft) high; dull lilac-colored flowers bloom in late winter, after which leaves appear, kidney shaped, 30 cm-150 cm (1-5 ft) in diameter, lighter below than above.

Decoction of root once used as a stimulant.

Caffeine Nut see Kola Tree.

Calamint *(Calamintha*

officinalis) 30 cm (1 ft). Small, pale blue flowers in July; leaves stalked, egg-shaped, and slightly serrated; square, hairy, woody stalks; strong scent.

Medicinal use of whole plant as an expectorant and to promote perspiration.

Cannabis *(Cannabis sativa)* 1-3 m (3-10 ft). Small and green flowers; narrow palm-like leaves from rough, angular, branched stems. Found wild in warm climates, but can be cultivated in temperate zones. Cultivation and use as drug is illegal.

Has considerable potential as an aid to psychotherapy and to aid opiate drug withdrawal. Legislation has to some extent suppressed development.

Capers *(Capparis spinosa)*. Taken from a shrub growing in the Mediterranean as unopened flower buds, which are pickled and used to flavor salads, sauces, etc.

Caraway *(Carum carvi)* 70-150 cm (2-5 ft). Small white or yellow flowers in compound umbels; fine, sheath-like leaves; characteristic hollow and furrowed stem; fruit oblong and dark brown. Found plentifully in temperate areas but also at arctic extremes. Culinary use of seeds for their pungent flavor in bread and cheeses.

Seed oil in herbal teas has been used to relieve chest colds; sometimes used to increase lactation; also to stimulate digestion.

Cardamom *(Eletteria cardamomum)* 2-5 m (6-16 ft). Small yellowish flowers from a tall erect stem, giving three-celled seed capsules. Found in southern India but cultivated in other tropical areas.

Culinary use of seeds in Indian cookery, ground in curry powder.

Caraway

Medicinal use in flavoring medicines but also as a mild stimulant.

Carnation *(Dianthus caryophyllum)*. Familiar plant grown for flowers; found in herb gardens for many years; useful to preserve fragrance.

Cassene see Cassina

Cassia *(Cinnamomum cassia)* (Chinese cinnamon). From the aromatic bark of a tree grown in tropical areas. Bark much thicker than true cinnamon and used in ground form as a substitute in flavoring cooking, in general, and particularly liqueurs and chocolate.

Cassina *(Ilex vomitoria)*
(Cassene Indian Black Drink).
Small evergreen tree or shrub;
bark whitish-gray; leathery
leaves. Leaves have been used
as tea for mild stimulant, and
a narcotic in stronger form.
Berries are poisonous.
Infusions used by North
American Indians as
ceremonial drink.

Catmint see Catnip

Catnip *(Nepeta cataria)*
(Catmint) 1-2 m (3-6.5 ft).
Flowers white with purple
spots growing in spikes
June-September; oblong,
pointed leaves with scalloped
edges and grey or whitish hairs
on the lower side; erect
branching stem. Easily grown in
most temperate gardens.

Tea claimed to cure
upset stomachs.

Cayenne *(Capsicum
frutescens)* 1 m (3 ft). Drooping
white to yellow flowers grow
alone or in twos or threes,
April-September; stem woody
near bottom and branched at
top; fruit, or pepper, is many-
seeded pod, leathery on
outside, in various shades of red
or yellow. Grown as an annual
in temperate climates but as a
perennial in tropical America.

Medicinal use of the pod
in powder form is one of the
finest body purifiers and internal
disinfectants known to man,
warding off infectious diseases
and colds.

Culinary use to provide hot
spicy flavors.

Celandine *(Chelidonium majus)*
(Great Celandine) 50-150 cm
(20-60 in). Bright yellow
flowers, with four petals
growing in a sparse umbel;
lobed leaflets; hollow stem,
round, smooth, and swollen at
joints; cylindrical red-brown
root. Plant contains
orange-yellow juice, which
turns red on exposure to air.

Juice once used as a
mild sedative on central
nervous system, relieving pain
and raising blood pressure;
also for gall bladder disorders.
Fresh juice is used to
remove warts.

Celery *(Apium graveolens)*
30-100 cm (1-3 ft). Familiar
vegetable plant; white flowers;
leaflets growing out of angular,
furrowed, branched stem;
fleshy bulbous root. Found
wild in damp places near sea,
and easily cultivated in gardens.

Culinary use in soups,
sauces, and stews, adding
strength if added at last moment.
Juice has been used for lack
of appetite; also to promote
onset of menstruation. Thought
to clear up skin problems, and
is therefore useful eaten in
salad, and made into tea.

Centaury *(Centaurium
confertum)* 15-50 cm (6-20 in).
Rose-colored, funnel-shaped
flowers June-September;
leaves at base oval in rosette;
higher stem leaves tending
to oblong; stem square,
hollow when older, branched
near top. Flowers once used
medicinally for many
complaints, chiefly as an aid
to digestion and as a lotion for
skin problems. Tea has been
recommended for those
leading sedentary lives.

Chamomile *(Anthemis nobilis)*.
Roman chamomile can grow to
40 cm (16 in) though 16 cm
(6 in) is more usual. Has a
yellow concave center to the
flower with white florets; is
found on the fringe of wheat
fields; can be sown early in
spring or autumn. Has been
observed to have a healing effect
on other plants in a garden.

Flowers have been used as
tea to aid digestion, having a
cleaning disinfectant effect;
also as a mouthwash after
dental treatment.

Chervil *(Anthriscus cerefolium)*
30-60 cm (12-24 in). Small
white flowers in compound
umbels; round, finely grooved,
branched stem. Best sown in
August and then monthly from
January. Also quite possible
in window boxes.

Culinary use for many years.
Mild flavor means generous
use necessary. Wide range
of applications.

Chestnut *(Aseculus
hippocastanum)* (Horse
Chestnut). Tree found widely,
giving familiar chestnut
as fruit.

Medicinal preparations from
fruit are important in treatment
of varicose veins and
hemorrhoids; dispensed only
by prescription. Flowers and
bark also used.

Chickweed *(Stelleria media)*
10-30 cm (4-12 in). Small white
flowers; smooth, egg-shaped,
sharp pointed leaves, brittle

Chickweed

creeping stems. A common weed, found all over the world in gardens and waste areas.

Culinary use as a vegetable like spinach. Fresh leaves, when crushed, are claimed to ease bruising.

Chicory *(Cichorium intybus)* 1 m (3 ft). Light-blue to violet-blue flower heads. July-October; lance-like leaves, coarsely toothed; stiff, angular, branching stem; yellow root. Plant contains bitter, milky juice. Cultivated and found wild in rich temperate grassy areas. Culinary use cooked or raw in salads.

Juice of leaves, used as a tea, claimed to promote production of bile, release of gallstones and elimination of excessive internal mucus.

Chinese Cinnamon see Cassia
Chives *(Allium schoenoprasum)* 10-24 cm (4-10 in). Grass-like cylindrical leaves; globular pale mauve flowers, if allowed; tiny bulb root. In fact a small onion (see Onion Green) but available earlier in year. Easily grown indoors and out, but particularly enjoy humidity. About the most satisfactory to grow.

Culinary use imparts mild onion flavor and has a wide range of applications.

Cicely see Sweet Cicely
Cinchona *(Rubiaceae* many species). Tree found in South America on eastern slopes of Andean highlands (tropical); also established in India, Sri Lanka and Java. The bark yields quinine, an important drug. Medicinally used for curing of malaria.

Cinnamon *(Cinnamomum zeylanicum)*. Small tropical evergreen laurel coming mainly from Sri Lanka and India. The bark is peeled off, dried, and ground.

Culinary use for spicy flavor in drinks, fruit, baked goods.

Cinquefoil *(Potentilla reptans)*. Ground-creeping, slender stem, rooting frequently, with long-stalked five-toothed leaves; golden-yellow flowers June-September, with five petals alternated with green sepals; roots are long and black.

Medicinal use of powdered root and leaves as gargle and mouthwash; also thought to be a remedy for diarrhea.

Clary see Sage
Cleavers see Clivers
Clivers *(Galium aparine)* (Cleavers) 60-180 cm (24-72 in). Small white flowers in flat-topped clusters; rough oblong leaves in whorls of six or eight around stem; slender root. Found in moist, grassy places.

Medicinal use of tea from juice or dried plant was once recommended for skin problems, and for healing wounds.

Clover *(Trifolium pratense)* (Red Clover). Up to 70 cm (28 in). Purplish-red globular flowers; oval leaflets with distinctive white bands; reddish stems. Often found wild but also cultivated, particularly for fodder.

Tea from flowers has been used for constipation and sluggish appetite. Poultice of plant for skin problems.

Cloves *(Caryophyllus aromaticus)* 5-10 m (16-32 ft). Tree with red and white bell-shaped flowers in terminal clusters; oval leaves. Dried bud is familiar clove. From Spice Islands, Philippines, and West Indies.

Culinary use in soups and stews and sweet dishes.

Medicinal use of oil or tea to soothe and act as an antiseptic.

Coca *(Erythroxylum coca)* 2.5 m (8 ft). Small, yellowish-white flowers in clusters; thin, oval, opaque leaves in straight branches. Resembles a blackthorn bush. Found in

western South America in hot damp conditions.

Medicinal use of leaves as a stimulant, usually by chewing. Source of cocaine. Internal action similar to opium, though less narcotic.

Coltsfoot *(Tussilago farfara)*. Creeping root, sending up downy white stems topped by large yellow flowers; large leaves, downy underneath. Found particulary on loamy, moist soils in hedgerows and waste areas. Leaves and flowers have been used in infusions and teas for treating colds and coughs and in compresses for treatment of varicose veins and some rashes.

Comfrey *(Symphytum officinale)* 60-100 cm (24-39 in). Cream or purple bell-like flowers;large hairy leaves have wavy edges; hairy stems; root black. Found in damp places by rivers.

Comfrey

Medicinal use of root in decoctions valuable as general tonic for bones and tendons. Is claimed to give relief to rheumatic pains if taken over a long period. Root in baths is said to be good for skin and in a poultice for bruises and insect bites.

Coriander *(Coriandrum sativum)* 30-70 cm (12-28 in). White flowers in umbels; round stems; lower leaves like parsley, upper leaves sharper. Unripe seeds smell horrible. Brought to Britain by the Romans. Found today on waste ground and also cultivated, especially in the USSR.

Culinary use of leaves, which have a bitter taste, and seeds, which dried have sage-like taste.

Medicinal use on wide scale of fruit in ointments for rheumatism and arthritis. Oil stimulates digestive secretions; also used in the perfume industry.

Cornflower *(Centuarea cyanus)* 30-60 cm (12-24 in). Little blue flowers in florets; long, thin leaves; thin, stiff branched stem. Found growing wild, but less frequently since chemical fertilizers. Often close to poppies.

Medicinal use of tea as an eyewash, and for cosmetic purposes.

Cowslip *(Primula veris)* 30-70 cm (12-28 in). Yellow flowers resemble tiny primrose heads all on one stem; slightly leathery leaves; erect central stem. Found in pastures, particularly on chalk.

Medicinal use of flowers in preparations as a sedative and as an expectorant.

Crocus see Autumn Crocus

Cubeb *(Piper cubeba)*. Vine or shrub growing in East Indies. Flowers grow in scaly spikes, developing into clusters of berries, resembling black

pepper, that are picked unripe and dried.

Medicinal use to relieve hay fever and asthma. Oil acts as antiseptic against gonorrhea.

Cumin *(Cuminum cyminum)* 30-60 cm (12-24 in). Small yellow flowers in clusters, grouped on branching stalks from branched stem, which is stiff and grooved.

Culinary use in curry powders but also with wide range of dishes, especially cheese dishes. Similar to caraway. Once used as a tea to aid digestion. Use of oil in perfumes.

Curry Powder Not derived from a single plant; is a blended mixture of various spices such as cardamom, cayenne, cloves, coriander, cumin, dill, fenugreek, ginger, mace, pepper, and turmeric. There is no standard recipe.

Daisy *(Bellis Perennis)* 10-20 cm (4-8 in). Familiar white flowers (often tinged with rose) with yellow center; soft hairy stems; fibrous root. Cultivated but commonly found wild on lawns and in meadows and other grassy places.

Medicinal use of flowers and leaves in tea for stomach and intestinal problems. Fresh flowers will help swelling and burns.

Damiana *(Turnera aphrodisiaca)*. Small shrub growing in Texas and northern Mexico. Leaves can be obtained from herbalists.

Medicinal use as a laxative and tonic. Supposed to be good for nervous and sexual debility; hence reputed aphrodisiac qualities.

Dandelion *(Taraxacum officinale)* 5-30 cm (2-12 in). Familiar yellow flowers on hollow, fleshy, rubbery, leafless stems; toothed leaves around base. Though often found as

weeds, can be cultivated if kept under control.

Culinary use of young leaves in salad or on sandwiches; highly nutritious, especially in Vitamin A (better than spinach). Dried leaves as general herb; dried, roasted root as coffee substitute. Has been used to improve gallbladder function and to stimulate digestion glands; also to combat rheumatism and gout.

Dill *(Anethum graveolens)* 90 cm (35 in). Flat clusters of tiny yellow flowers; leaves feathery; finely serrated erect stem with alternate white and green stripes; fruit oval. Found wild, but widely cultivated. Needs well-drained soil and sunny position. Sow continuously April-June. Grow away from fennel.

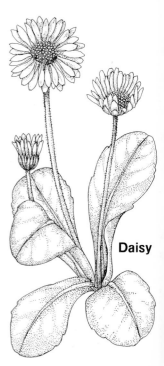

Daisy

78

Culinary use of leaves for flavoring, particularly fish, bland vegetables and pickled cucumbers; seeds, in soups.

Seeds have been used as tea for vomiting and hiccups; chewing of seed is useful for halitosis.

Dock *(Rumex hydrolapathum)* Water Dock) 2m (6 ft). Small greenish-yellow flowers with white heads; hollow branched stem; narrow elliptical leaves; large reddish-brown roots. Largest of dock family is found near rivers, ditches and ponds, and in marshy places. Use of roots believed to be a general body cleanser.

Elder *(Sambucus nigra)* 2.5-9 m (8-30 ft). Small white and yellowish flowers with heavy scent; dark green leaves; shiny black-violet fruit. Shrub or tree found frequently; requires control to prevent undue spreading.

Culinary use of berries in jam, juices, and wines and of flowers in jam tarts and milk dishes.

Flowers once used as sleep-inducing tea and for rheumatism. Fruits said to produce perspiration, reducing fever; also said to have an effect on chronic catarrh. Elderflower water can be used for eye and skin lotions and as a mild astringent. Tea bags, for tea and water, can be purchased in health-food stores.

Elecampane *(Inula Helenium)* 1-2 m (3-6 ft). Large yellow flowers; olive-colored leaves; stout, round, coarse stem; fibrous root, brown-white color inside. Grows wild in many areas; sometimes cultivated.

Root has been used medicinally to ease coughing, and in treatment for diabetes; also in herbal teas for gallbladder treatment. Used as mouthwash for sore gums.

Distilled oil is used in perfume manufacture.
English Mace see Mace
Eucalyptus *(Eucalyptus globulus)*. Tall evergreen tree found in Australia, Tasmania, and the USA.

Medicinal use of oil of mature leaves for treatment of lung diseases, colds, and sore throats. Commonly found in cough drops. Used externally as an antiseptic.

European Mandrake see Mandrake
Eyebright *(Euphrasia officinalis)* 30 cm (12 in). Purple and white flowers; square, leafy stem. Very common in pastures and other grassy areas.

Medicinal use for curing eye infections, using weak infusion of the fresh herb; has been used as a tea for gallbladder disorders.
Fennel *(Foeniculum vulgare)* 60-130 cm (24-50 in). Flat, golden-yellow flowers in umbels; leaves much divided, light green when young, getting darker; short, erect stem, striated and polished. Often found wild. Easy to cultivate; likes rich, chalky soil and warm location. Relative of dill.

Culinary use of chopped leaves in sauces and on fish; aids digestion. Compresses steeped in tea have been used on eyes for inflammation. Seed oil has been used as a disinfectant.
Fenugreek *(Trigonella toenumgraecum)*. Yellowish flowers; round stem with few branches; seeds contained in a pod. Member of the pea family. Found in dry, sandy places.

Culinary use of seeds as an aromatic and in general cooking.

Medicinal use as a tonic and for bronchitis and tuberculosis.
Feverfew *(Chrysanthemum foenum-graecum)* 50 cm (20 in). Daisy-like flowers with

Green Hellebore

yellow centers and white petals; deeply cut, yellowish-green leaves; round, leafy, branching stem. Grows wild in hedges and on banks, or can be cultivated.

Medicinally once popular in infusions for indigestion, colds, and alcoholic D.T.s Flowers as a purgative.
Flax see Linseed
Foxglove *(Digitalis purpurea)* 70-150 cm (28-60 in). Bell-shaped flowers, rose/purple color on outside, white with red spots inside; stout, simple, straight stem, with alternate downy leaves. Cultivated and found wild, especially on the edge of woodland.

Leaves are used to make heart stimulant, but are **poisonous.**

Galangal *(Alpinia galanga)* 1-1.5 m (3-5 ft). White flowers in clusters growing from procumbent stem; creeping root, cylindrical and branched, ringed with old leaf sheaths. Odor and taste of root is like ginger. Found wild and cultivated in China, southeast Asia, Indonesia, and Iran.

Medicinally once used as ginger, a hot tea promoting cleansing perspiration.

Garlic *(Allium sativum)* 30-50 cm (12-20 in). Round umbel of small white flowers; stem simple, smooth, and round, surrounded at the bottom by tubular leaf sheaths; bulb is composed of multiple cloves. Widely cultivated. Every clove planted will produce a whole bulb.

Culinary use for a wide range of dishes.

Medicinal use to stimulate digestion; said to be especially beneficial to the blood.

Gentian see Alpine Gentian
Ginger *(Zingiber officinale)* 100-130 cm (39-51 in). White flowers with purple streaks, growing in spikes; long, oval leaves from simple leafy stem, with leaf sheath around base; knotty root, fibrous and buff-colored

Medicinal use of aromatic root as tea or syrup provides soothing remedy for coughs; tea provides refreshing gargle.

Culinary use in a variety of cuisines, particularly eastern.

Ginseng *(Panax schin-seng).* Small plant coming almost exclusively from eastern Asia, where it is cultivated. (*Pa. quinquefolius* is grown in USA and is similar). The aromatic root may grow to a length of 70 cm (28 in).

Medicinal use of the ground root is held to be useful for the relief of many ailments; it also acts as a stimulant on

Heartsease

the central nervous system.
Goldenrod see Solidago
Golden Seal *(Hydrastis canadensis)* 30 cm (12 in). Solitary flower at top of erect stem with two five-lobed leaves; thick, knotty, yellow root. Found in rich woods and meadows.

Medicinal use of ground root to clear catarrhal conditions. Apply tea with toothbrush for sore gums. Do not eat fresh plant.
Great Celandine see Celandine
Green Hellebore *(Helleborus viridis).* Up to 30 cm (12 in). Branched stem with large white flowers each with own leaf. Found mainly in alpine forests but also in some gardens.

Has been used medicinally for stimulation of the heart.

Warning: contact with bruised herb may cause dermatitis.
Ground Ivy *(Nepeta hedracea).* Creeping plant with bluish-purple, two-lipped flowers; fine-haired stem with root nodes along entire length.

Leaves and flowers have been used to relieve diarrhea, colds, and bronchitis; but in large quantities can be poisonous.
Groundsel *(Senecio vulgaris)* 30-70 cm (12-28 in). Golden-yellow flowers with brown centers; coarse-toothed leaves at base; erect, grooved, brown-streaked stem. Found in wet areas, in marshes, along stream-banks, and generally in waste areas.

The whole plant has been used for liver complaints, but never without medical supervision. Used by the Indians for abortion. Known to be poisonous to livestock.
Hawkweed *(Hieracium pilosella)* 10-40 cm (4-16 in). Solitary yellow flower heads on bristly stems; creeping leafy runners; leaves also bristly. Found in dry soil on lawns, in pastures, etc.

Tea supposed to be a cure for diarrhea; used also as a gargle for sore throats.
Hawthorne *(Crataegus monogyna).* Familiar shrub or tree with thorny branches. White flowers and red fruit — the "haw."

Medicinal use in drug industry of flowers and berries for cardiac disorders of nervous origin. Beneficial in treatment after a stroke.

Culinary use of leaf to make tea as a substitute for Oriental green tea.
Heartsease *(Viola tricolor)* (Wild Pansy) 30-50 cm (12-20 in). Solitary flowers — yellow, blue, violet, or two-colored; angular, soft, hollow stem with alternate toothed leaves. Widely

cultivated on gardens, but also found in fields and at the edge of woods.

Has been used in herbal teas for relief of catarrh and in treatment of rheumastism. Large doses can lead to skin problems.

Hemlock *(Conium maculatum)* ½-2 m (2-6 ft). Large umbels of small, white flowers; seeds grey-green; smooth purple-spotted stem, branching at the top. Found in all sorts of waste areas.

All parts of this herb are dangerous poison. Used in classical times to execute criminals. **Dangerous.**

Henbane *(Hyoscyamus niger)* 30-70 cm (12-28 in). Dull yellow or beige flowers with purple veins; hairy leaves and stem, which is sticky. Has a strong smell; also known as Stinking Nightshade. Found in waste areas, particularly on chalk. Long cultivated for medical purposes.

Medicinal use of oil from leaves as cure for earache and rheumatism, but only under medical direction. The whole plant is **poisonous.**

Henna *(Lawsonia inermis)*. Small shrub growing in Arabia, North Africa, Iran, and the East Indies. Grayish-green leaves and fragrant red flowers.

Medicinal use of leaves to make a soothing gargle. Often used for dying hair.

Herb Bennet *(Geum urbanum)*. Up to 30 cm (12 in). Five-petaled yellow flowers; hairy, erect stem. Found in hedgerows and in deciduous forests. Grown as a potherb in the 16th century.

Root extract has been used to promote digestion; flowers, as a gargle. Once thought to repel moths.

Culinary use in broths and soups.

Herb Robert *(Geranium robertianum)* 30-70 cm (12-28 in). Purplish-red or rose-colored flowers; petals have long "claws." Reddish stem is hairy, thick, juicy, and forked. Found in rocky woodland.

Herb has been used medicinally for diarrhea, enteritis, and gout and as a hot poultice of boiled leaves for bruises and skin problems.

Holly *(Ilex aquifolium)*. Common tree or shrub with shiny, leathery prickly leaves and bright red berries.

Medicinal use of leaves not common, but once considered good for gout, rheumatism, and arthritis. The berries are mildly poisonous and are dangerous to children.

Honeysuckle *(Lonicera periclymenum)*. Creeping stem 3-7 m (10-23 ft). Yellow flowers tinged with red, rich in

Horseradish

nectar, sweet scent; tough stem; leaves in pairs. Found growing widely in hedges, and often trained up the sides of houses.

Culinary use of flowers to make syrup; can be eaten raw; sweet tasting.

Has been used as a tonic for the heart; also for chest colds and coughs and glandular ailments.

Hops *(Humulus lupulus)*. Climbing vine, stems often reaching 6 m (20 ft). Yellowish-green flowers; "hops" are the scaly, cone-like fruit; stems and leaves rough. Found growing wild and widely cultivated.

Culinary use chiefly to flavor beer, but not generally accepted until the 15th century. Use of tea for insomnia (also hop pillows) and for digestion.

Horehound *(Marrubium vulgare)* (White Horehound) 30-100 cm (12-40 in). Small, white, two-lipped flowers; wrinkled leaves; numerous bushy, square, downy stems. Found in waste areas.

Medicinally has been used as a remedy for coughing and bronchial problems. Tea or crushed leaves for persistent skin problems.

Horse Chestnut see Chestnut

Horseradish *(Armoracia rusticana)* 1 m (3 ft). Small white flowers on short stalks growing from thick stem; crinkly, palm-like leaves, with characteristic smell when crushed; long, thick root. Very common on waste ground, though many people fail to recognize it.

Culinary use of shredded root to make traditional sauce for use with meats. Root contains mustard oil and Vitamin C.

Medicinal use of root, grated or as syrup, supposed to relieve bronchial catarrh.

Horsetail *(Equisetum arvense)* 10-15 cm (4-6 in). Fertile, flesh-colored stem, with spike containing spores. Taller stem grows later with whorls of small branches. Found wild in moist, loamy, or sandy soils.

Medicinal use of herb once claimed to cure lung problems; the silicic acid content said to stabilize scar tissue. Tea is used to wash wounds. Large doses are poisonous.

Hyssop *(Hyssopus officinalis).* Bushy evergreen plant, with several downy stems, woody at the bottom; rose to bluish-purple flowers. Mainly found as ornamental plant today, but once widely cultivated for medicinal use.

Medicinally has been used for a variety of ailments; a great cleanser (Bible: "purge me with hyssop"). Use crushed leaves on wounds to prevent infection and promote healing.

Indigo *(Indigofera sumatrana).* A plant cultivated in the East for many centuries. Important for its purple dye, which is resistant to fading. Major commercial cultivation in India until the turn of the century, when development of synthetic alternative caused economic crisis.

Iris Florentina *(Iris florentina)* (Orris Root). Flowers white with blue veins, outer divisions fringed with yellow; sword-like leaves from base; erect stem. Comes from Mediterranean, but often cultivated in cooler climates. Orris root is, in fact, the root-stock. Commercial production is centered in Florence.

Medicinal use of root for treatment of dropsy and similar problems. Sometimes used for sore throats and coughs. Also used in making pomanders.

Ivy *(Hedera Helix).* Evergreen climber common everywhere.

Leaves vary in shape. Trunk may reach 30 cm (12 in) in diameter after long growth.

Medicinal use of leaves once made as wash for sores, burns, etc. Leaves may cause dermatitis. Also thought to break down red blood corpuscles.

Jasmine *(Jasminum officinale).* Vine-like plant with sweet smelling white flowers and plentiful dark-green leaves. Found in warm parts of the eastern hemisphere.

Medicinal use of oil in India to treat snake-bites.

Perfume ingredients often include jasmine oil, which is very expensive.

Juniper *(Juniperus communis).* Small, graceful evergreen shrub up to 3.5 m (11 ft). Needle-like leaves; reddish stems; small yellow flowers; red berries take two to three years to ripen. Often found growing in old gardens or can be cultivated. Use of berries, which contain valuable oils, to stimulate appetite and dissolve mucus.

Culinary use in making conserve, or for tea. Also in flavoring gin and liqueurs.

Khus-Khus *(Vetiveria zizanioides)* 2 m (7 ft). Tall, perennial grass growing in large clumps. Long, narrow, rough leaves; spiky flowers. Found in tropical and sub-tropical Asia and East Indies.

Culinary use of root to make a stimulating tea.

Kidney Vetch *(Anthyllis vulneraria)* 20-40 cm (8-16 in). Yellow flowers in clover-like heads; leaflets on erect stem. Found wild in limestone soils.

Flowering tops have been used to make infusion for washing wounds and as a tea for a mild purgative.

Kidneywort see Pennywort

Knapweed *(Centuarea scabiosa)* 30-70 cm (12-28 in).

Lettuce

Globular flower heads with cottony scales and bright purple florets; long leaves in segments; grooved, slightly branched stem, covered in soft hairs. Found in dry waste places, often close to thistles.

Medicinally has been used in the treatment of glandular disorders; also to relieve catarrh. The flowers and root were used.

Culinary use of flowers in salads.

Kola Tree *(Cola acuminata)* (Caffeine nut). Tree growing wild in Africa and cultivated in South America and the West Indies. Fruit is yellowish-brown woody pod containing white or red nuts.

Medicinal use of nuts as a stimulant. Nuts contain more caffeine than coffee berries.

Ladies Bedstraw *(Calium verum)* 30-70 cm (12-28 in).

Mass of tiny yellow flowers smelling of honey; feathery leaves; slender stem. Found wild in hedgerows. When dried, develops characteristic hay-like smell.

Culinary use in curdling milk into junkets and cheese.

Lad's Love see Southernwood

Lady's Mantle *(Alchemilla vulgaris)* 10-50 cm (4-20 in). Small green flowers in loose clusters; 7-8 lobed leaves at base, with some finely toothed; stem starts green, then changes to blue-green and to reddish or brownish. Can be easily grown, but must be kept under tight control. Also found in shady woods and damp places.

Medicinally has been used in the treatment of all manner of women's disorders.

Lavender *(Lavandula officinalis* etc.). Common shrub, often cultivated in gardens for its aromatic flowers. Lilac-colored flowers in multiple whorls; gray-green leaves.

Medicinal use of oil derived from flowers by distillation with water. Used for headaches, particularly migraine, fainting, and dizziness. Also as an antiseptic.

Lemon Balm see Balm
Lemon Verbena see Verbena
Leopards Bane see Arnica
Lettuce *(Lactuca virosa).* The common lettuce consumed in salads is the half-grown form of this herb. When allowed to mature ("bolt"), a tall stem develops with alternative leaves and heads of yellow flowers.

Medicinal use has been made of milky juice as lactucarium, which is a mild opium substitute used in laudanum.

Licorice *(Glycyrrhiza glabra)* 30-70 cm (12-28 in). Spike of yellowish or purplish flowers; oval, dark green leaflets; stem rounded in lower part but angular higher up; woody, wrinkled root tasting sweet. Cultivated in some parts, but often found wild.

Medicinal use of the root for bronchial problems and mucous congestion and as the orthodox drug for stomach disorders. A strong decoction makes a good laxative for children. Added to other medicines to make them more palatable.

Used in the candy industry. The root is often chewed by children.

Lily of the Valley *(Convallaria majalis)* 30 cm (12 in). Bell-shaped white flowers on single stem between two oblong, pointed leaves that sheath the base of the stem. Found wild, but usually cultivated in gardens.

Medicinal use as ointment for headaches and rheumatism; and under medical supervision as a cardiac agent. **Poisonous.**

Linseed *(Linum usitatissimum)* (Flax) 50-100 cm (20-40 in). Blue or violet-blue flowers; erect, slender stem with numerous narrow oblong leaves. The fruit is an 8-10 seeded capsule; seeds are smooth, flattened, shiny, and light brown. Found alongside roads and railways, but also widely cultivated especially in the USA.

Seeds have been used to make decoction for coughs, lung and chest problems; the oil, for the removal of gallstones; and the seeds, intact for constipation.

Liverwort see Agrimony

Lovage *(Ligusticum officinalis)* 1-2 m (3-6.5 ft). Plentiful greenish-yellow flowers; incised and oval leaves; straight, round, hollow stem; strong fleshy roots. Easy to grow, and also found wild.

Culinary use in soups, casseroles, stocks, stews, etc. Has a yeasty flavor that imparts strength to other flavors. Leaves also used as a vegetable.

Mace see Nutmeg

Madder *(Rubia tinctorum).* Creeping root sends up climbing stems that may be found lying prostrate. Flowers small and yellow-green; leaves in whorls around stem; cylindrical, reddish-brown root. Found growing in Mediterranean countries, where it is also cultivated.

Medicinally claimed to prevent stones in the kidneys and bladder when taken as powdered root. Decoction was also once used for skin problems.

Much use of cultivated madder in the dye industry.

Maidenhair *(Adiantum pedatum)* 1-1.5 m (3-5 ft). Fern leaflets (3-8) on each stem that forks from the main stem. Found wild in moist, cool places.

Mallow

Decoction made from leaves has been used for coughs and congestion caused by colds. Sometimes used as a hair tonic.
Mallow *(Malva sylvestris/ rotundifolia)* (High/Low Mallow). Both have pink or purple flowers with 5-7 lobes and light green, downy leaves with 5-7 lobes. High variety grows to 1 m (3 ft) on erect stem; low variety is a creeper with branching stem up to 70 cm (28 in) long. Both are found in waste areas and also cultivated.

Both herbs have been used medicinally as a tea for coughs and hoarseness. External use of decoction for wounds and sores.
Mandrake *(Mandragora officinarum)* (European Mandrake). Bell-shaped flowers on short stems; oval leaves grow erect but then lie flat on the ground; large brown root growing 1-1.5 m (3-5 ft) deep. The fruit is a large, fleshy, yellow-orange berry. Found largely in countries round the Mediterranean.

Medicinally used today in the treatment of asthma and coughs, but is poisonous. In ancient times was used as an anesthetic, which could be fatal.
Marigold *(Calendula officinalis)* 30-70 cm (12-28 in). Large, yellow or orange terminal flowers; leaves hairy with widely spaced teeth. Easily grown in the garden and commonly seen everywhere.

Medicinal use of the leaves and flowers claimed for stomach and intestinal complaints or as a salve for wounds.

Culinary use to add a pleasant flavor to stews, etc.; also used in salads. Flowers and leaves can both be used.
Marjoram *(Origanum majorana/onites/vulgare)* (Sweet Marjoram/Pot M./Wild M. — Oregano). All three grow with a bush-like appearance about 25 cm (10 in). high with flowering stems growing higher in Pot M. variety. Flowers are mauve, pink, or light red; stems are woody. All can be cultivated. The Pot M. variety is easiest for the gardener but not as flavorful.

Culinary use of each of these species is common. Sweet marjoram is gentler than oregano, which is quite spicy, especially in the Mediterranean variety.
Marshmallow *(Althea officinalis)* 70-120 cm (28-47 in). Light red, white, or purple flowers; unbranched, woody stems; white, sweet-tasting root. Found in wet places and also cultivated.

Medicinal use of infusion of leaves as a soothing gargle; external use for irritations, burns, carbuncles, and wounds. Mix grated root with honey for healing poultice.
Meadowsweet *(Filipendula ulmaria)* 70-120 cm (28-47 in). Small yellowish-white or reddish flowers; three- or five-lobed terminal leaflets; reddish angular stem, branched near the top. Common in damp meadows.

Medicinal use of whole plant, which contains salicylic acid, useful for influenza, gout, rheumatism etc. The tea is reported to be good for dropsy and bladder and kidney ailments.
Mimosa *(Mimosa Acacia etc.)*. Wide number of species in shrub, tree, and creeper forms. Found widely in tropical and subtropical areas. Flowers used in production of scent.
Mint There are a wide variety of mints used in cooking and for their fragrance. It is well worth cultivating a small collection of them.
Apple Mint *(Mentha rotundifolia)*. Contains the flavor of apples, as well as the true mint.
Black Peppermint *(Mentha piperita)*. Used for making tea and commercially for distilling peppermint oil.
Bowles Mint *(Mentha rotundifolia,Bowles variety)*. Has thick, fleshy leaves and is excellent for mint sauce; a robust species.
Curly Mint *(Mentha spicata & Mentha crispa)*. Very hardy, used for mint omelets. Common in Germanic countries.
Eau de cologne Mint *Mentha citrata)*. Fragrant lemon mint used in scent, in potpourri and in drinks.
Pennyroyal *(Mentha pulegium)*. Used medicinally to alleviate a depressed state of mind. Once used to "purify" water.
Pineapple Mint *(Mentha rotundifolia variegata)*. A fragrant mint also used for drinks.
Spearmint *(Mentha viridis or Mentha spicata)*. The mint usually found in gardens; als called green mint and pea mint. The oil is used in flavoring chewing gum.
Water Mint *(Mentha aquatica)*. Used medicinally like pennyroyal.
White Peppermint *(Mentha piperita officinalis)*. Used in the same way as black peppermint.
Mistletoe *(Viscum album)*. An evergreen parasitic creeper found on the branches of deciduous trees. Roots growing from the yellow-green stem penetrate into the wood of the host; leathery leaves, yellow-green and oval; pale yellow or green flowers; sticky white berries.

Has medicinal effect of varying blood pressure; large doses are harmful. Tea can be used for bathing chilblains.
Mugwort *(Artemisia vulgaris)* 60-120 cm (24-48 in). Purple or dull-yellow flower heads;

dark leaves, white down beneath, divided into lobes; stems purplish-red; root woody. Found in waste areas and beside roads. Cultivation is easy on any kind of soil.

Culinary use as an aromatic herb in salads and for seasoning fish and meat.

Medicinally has been used against chronic diarrhea and for diabetics. Makes a soothing footbath.

Mulberry *(Morus nigra).* Tree growing up to 25 m (82 ft) high.

Medicinal use of the bark for tapeworms; milky juice in leaves for ringworm. The juice and unripe fruit can cause hallucinations and stomach upset.

Ripe fruit is delicious to eat and can be made into jam.

Mullein *(Verbascum thapsiforme)* 1-1.5 m (3-5 ft). Tall, stout stem with alternate, thick, felt-like leaves, light green color; yellow flowers in cylindrical spikes.

Flowers have been used for coughs and mucous congestion and externally for inflammations and painful skin conditions.

Mustard Black Mustard *(Brassica nigra).* White Mustard *(Brassica hirta).* Both have yellow flowers and the seeds in pods. Black M. is taller (up to 2 m-6.5 ft) than White M. (1 m-3 ft), both have angular, branched stems.

Medicinal use of seed to treat rheumatism and various internal inflammations. Undiluted oil is dangerous to the skin.

Culinary use to prepare familiar condiment.

Nasturtium *(Tropaeolum majus, T. minus).* Strong climbing plant, also developed as a non-climber. Leaves kidney-shaped and flowers yellow, orange, red, and brownish. Native of South America, but widely grown and very prolific.

Culinary use of leaves in sandwiches and spreads imparting a peppery flavor. Also use of seeds and flowers. High vitamin C content in the leaves.

Nettle *(Urtica dioica, U. urens).* The former is the stinging nettle, the latter is smaller and greener. Both have heart-shaped leaves. Exceedingly common, hardly requiring cultivation.

Culinary use of young shoots, which have a delicate flavor when treated like spinach.

Medicinal use of fresh juice reported to stimulate digestion and to promote lactation. Do not eat old leaves uncooked as they can cause kidney damage.

Nasturtium

Nutmeg *(Myristica fragans).* Mace is the seed covering; nutmeg, the seed. Tropical evergreen tree found in the West Indies, Indonesia, and South America.

Culinary use of both as spice.

Medicinal use as a hallucinogenic similar to marijuana. Eating as few as two nutmegs can cause death.

Oak *(Quercus robur).* The common tree with the familiar leaves and acorns.

Bark has been used in treatment of intestinal catarrh and diarrhea and for treatment of frostbite and rashes. Acorn formerly used as an antidote to poisoning.

Culinary use of roasted acorns as coffee substitute; when raw, is rather bitter. Acorns used in tanning industry.

Olive *(Olea europaea).* Evergreen tree native to the Mediterranean but cultivated in other subtropical areas. Gray-green bark; leathery leaves; shiny black fruit when ripe.

Culinary use of olives eaten whole or as oil.

Medicinal use of oil as a laxative and externally for burns Decoction of leaves or inner bark effective against fever.

Onion, Green *(Allium fistulosum)* (Welsh Onion) 15-30 cm (6-12 in). Circular section leaves; yellowish white flowers. A larger version of chives (cf), imparting a slightly stronger taste to cooking.

Opium Poppy *(Papaver somniferum).* Up to 50 cm (20 in). Single stems with terminal flowers, white and mauve in color; leaves, growing directly from stems, are crinkled; bulging seed pod. Grows wild and is cultivated around the Mediterranean.

Medicinal use of milky fluid from seeds as opium and

Peony

related drugs (e.g., codeine). All have a strong effect on pain, particularly morphine. All production is under international narcotic laws.

Orange *(Citrus aurantium).* The evergreen orange tree, cultivated in subtropical areas, producing bitter fruit suitable for making marmalade.

Medicinal use of the rind and flowers as a tonic and stimulant; also in making perfume.

Oregano see Marjoram
Orris Root see Iris Florentina
Pansy see Heartsease

Paprika *(Capsicum frutescens).* Another capsicum shrub, (see Cayenne). This is the largest and mildest, the ground pod being used mainly for decoration of food.

Parsley *(Carum petroselinum).* There are a number of different varieties: Curly, Hamburg, French, Italian, etc. Found in cultivation everywhere; not hard to grow, but germination can take a long time.

Culinary uses are numerous. Used during or after cooking, particularly with savory dishes.

Parsley is rich in vitamins A, B and C and in many minerals. Reported to stimulate the digestive glands and improve the working of the whole digestive system.

Pennywort *(Cotyledon umbilicus-veneris, Umbilicus rupestris)* (Kidneywort) 15 cm (6 in). Greenish-white flowers resembling bluebells from hollow flower stems; pale green, heart-shaped leaves. Found in rock crevices and in walls.

Whole plant has been used to make an astringent and to help liver and kidneys.

Peony *(Paeonia officinalis)* 70-100 cm (28-40 in). Large, solitary, red or purplish-red flowers; green, juicy stem; knobby root. Grows wild in southern Europe, and cultivated elsewhere.

Root has been used for jaundice, kidney, and gallbladder problems. Entire plant is poisonous, especially the flowers.

Pepper *(Piper nigrum)* (Black Pepper and White Pepper). Both are dried berries of the tropical pepper vine. The black comes from underripe berries that have been dried and cured; the white, from dried ripe berries whose dark outer shell has been removed. White

pepper is not as strong as black, but its flavor is finer and more aromatic.

Periwinkle *(Vinca major, V. minor).* Prostrate creeping plant with dark green shiny leaves at joints and a pale blue flower. Found wild and also cultivated.

Has been thought to be a good remedy for diarrhea, excessive menstruation and hemorrhage; also tea for soothing hysteria and fits.

Plantain *(Plantago major, P. lanceolata).* Both have spikes of greenish-white flowers, shorter in the latter case; the leaves differ totally, being oval in the former and lance-like in the latter. Both grow to about 50 cm (20 in), though *lanceolata* may double this height. Found in many waste areas.

Whole plant has been used as an astringent, a soother, and for kidney complaints.

Culinary use of young leaves as spinach; can be eaten raw, but rather bitter.

Primrose *(Primula officinalis)* 10-25 cm (4-10 in). Funnel-shaped yellow flowers; rosette of oval crenulated leaves. Found in gardens and many wild locations.

Medicinal use of infusions of flowers once used for general headaches, insomnia, and nervous conditions; oil from leaves for skin problems.

Culinary use of flowers in roast veal.

Purslane *(Portulaca oleracea)* (Green Purslane) 30-70 cm (12-28 in). Five-petaled yellow flowers; fat, thick leaves — round, smooth, reddish, and succulent; brittle stems. Can be grown, but often found wild.

Leaves and seeds have been used as a laxative and to treat intestinal worms.

Culinary use of leaves cooked whole

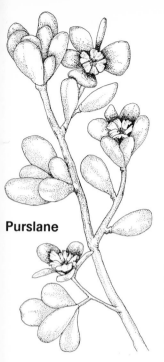
Purslane

All are the familiar bush or rambler marked by their prickly stems. Flowers are usually pale pink or white, fragrant, and with many yellow stamens.

Culinary use of rose hip tea or purée, as rich in vitamins C and A. Seeds are **dangerous** and can cause stomach hemorrhage.

Rosemary *(Rosmarinus officinalis)*. Up to 1.5 m (5 ft). Delicate blue flowers in clusters; succulent leaves, narrow like pine needles, green on top, grayish-green beneath; woody trunk with many branches. There are a number of different varieties that vary in size. Can be cultivated best on a light, sandy soil, preferably on chalk, as needs lime.

Medicinal use of tea supposed to be good for weak digestion and neuralgic pains; also stimulates the circulation.

Culinary use in wide variety of preparations including, soups, stews meat, fish. Particularly noted for its fragrance.

Rue *(Ruta graveolens)* 30-70 cm (2-28 in). Small yellow-green flowers growing in clusters; branched, pale green stem. Aromatic. Found wild, but usually cultivated.

Traditional medicinal use to relieve gout pains and to treat nervous heart problems. Large doses can cause **poisoning;** especially dangerous for pregnant women.

Safflower *(Carthamus tinctorius)* 30-100 cm (12-40 in). Orange-yellow flowers; branching stem; oval leaves with small, spiny teeth. Found wild, but often cultivated.

Flowers have been used to make tea, producing strong perspiration; used for colds etc. Also used for

Ragwort *(Senecio jacobaea)* 30-70 cm (12-28 in). Flowers with golden-yellow rays and brownish discs; erect, grooved, brown-streaked stem; coarse-toothed basal leaves. Found in wet areas, along stream banks and in marshes.

Traditional medicinal use for a variety of women's disorders. American Indians used it to speed abortion. Contains toxics dangerous to livestock.

Red Clover see Clover

Rose Geranium see Geranium

Rose Hips Dog Rose *(Rosa canina)*, Wild Rose *(Rosa rugosa)*, Sweetbriar *(Rosa rubiginosa)*. Rose hips are the red/orange fruit, berries that are left after the flowers wilt. Dog rose is the most common.

soothing hysteria.

Use of flowers – ground up and mixed with talcum powder – to make rouge.

Saffron *(Crocus sativus)* 30-70 cm (12-28 in). Funnel-shaped, reddish-purple flowers, growing with gray-green leaves from corm. Leaves have hairy margins and grow to height of whole plant. Widely cultivated.

Medicinal use of stamens from flowers for coughs, colic, and insomnia, but only in small doses. Rarely used, as very expensive. Can be highly **poisonous.**

Main use of cultivated flowers in dye and perfume manufacture. Also used for cooking, but high cost restricts usage.

Sage *(Salvia officinalis)* 60 cm (24 in). Violet-blue flowers, hardy, grayish-green leaves with serrated edges; strong woody stems; an undershrub. Grows wild in southern Europe, but usually cultivated.

Culinary use is extensive. Should be used sparingly, as it has a strong flavor. Helps digestion.

Medicinal use of tea for gargling and is supposed to reduce sweating. Prolonged dosing can be **poisonous.** Steambaths with added sage have cosmetic qualities.

St.-John's-Wort *(Hypericum perforatum)* 30-70 cm (12-28 in). Flat-topped, yellow flower clusters, petals dotted with black along the edges. The oblong/linear leaves are covered with transparent oil glands that look like holes. Round stems with runners at base. A shrubby plant with a turpentine-like odor. Found generally in dry gravelly soils.

Medicinal use of whole plant to treat wounds. All good herbal ointments contain St.-John's-

Wort. Oil extract for stomach and intestinal problems. Has sometimes poisoned livestock
Salad Burnet see Burnet
Savory Summer Savory *(Satureja hortensis).* Winter Savory *(Satureia montana)* Former is 30 cm (12 in), bushy plant, sparse leaves. Erect stem hairy and quadrangular, woody at base; narrow, dark green leaves; lilac, pink, or whitish flowers. Whole plant appears purplish. Latter is 15-40 cm (6-16 in) compact undershrub and similar but has silky bark and grayish-green leaves. Both are found wild, in the Mediterranean. In cultivation, summer savory prefers rich soil, but winter savory a poor and chalky one.

Culinary use of both in a variety of dishes and deserves some experimentation. The variety is not as delicate.

Medicinally has been used as tea for digestive problems, also as a gargle for sore throats.
Scarlet Pimpernel *(Anagallis arvensis).* Stems wander over surface to length of 30 cm (12 in); starlike red flowers; oval leaves blue-green on top, brown or black on underside. Found particularly on loamy soils.

Medicinally reputed to cause sweating and increased kidney activity. Acts on central nervous system and brain. Dangerous.
Senna *(Cassia acutifolia)* 1-2 m (3-6.5 ft). Yellow flowers in bunches; stems round and slightly hairy; each leaf divided into 8-10 leaflets. Found in North America also as another species in northern Africa.

Medicinal use of pods as a laxative. Use infusion for halitosis.
Sesame Seeds *(Sesamum indicum).* The seeds of an erect plant growing in tropical and subtropical areas. Many

varieties. One of the first oil seeds grown by man. Seeds contain 45-63% edible oil and 16-32% protein.

Culinary use of oil in salads, cooking, and in the manufacture of margarine.
Shepherd's Purse *(Capsella bursa-pastoris)* 15-50 cm (6-20 in). Small white flowers in flat-topped clusters; erect, simple branching stem; Common in fields and waste areas everywhere.

Extract has been used to stop internal and external bleeding; raises blood pressure.
Skullcap *(Scutellaria lateriflora)* 30-70 cm (12-28 in). Two-lipped pale purple or blue flowers; branching stem; serrated oval leaves come to a point; yellow root.

Medicinal use of infusions thought good for spasms and contractions. American Indians used it to promote menstruation.
Sloe see Buckthorne.
Snakeroot see Bistort.
Solidago *(Solidago virgaurea)* (Golden rod). Elongated flower clusters; hairy, round, striped stem; oblong leaves. Often found growing wild and in gardens. Very colorful when in flower.

Tea from leaves and flowers once used for arthritis, whooping cough, and chronic eczema. Said to be useful for kidney problems. Crushed fresh leaves for wounds, sores, and insect bites.
Sorrel *(Rumex acetosa)* (French Sorrel) 60 cm (24 in). Slender plant with juicy stems and leaves and whorled spikes of reddish-green flowers; leaves oblong, slightly arrow-shaped at the base, succulent. Common in damp meadows and along roads. Other varieties, all with same taste. Culinary use of fresh young

Sorrell

leaves cooked, preferably in combination. Particularly good for making soup.

An important vitamin C source. Large quantities can irritate kidneys and cause mild poisoning.
Southernwood *(Artemesia abrotanum)* (Lad's Love). This is a much safer herb than its relation wormwood or absinthe (cf), which it strongly resembles. This one has yellowish-white flowers.
Sphagnum Moss *(Sphagnum).* The chief component of peat bogs. Medicinal use as a cleansing and healing dressing.
Spikenard *(Nardostarchys jatamausi).* The true source of the valuable perfume is from the Indian species.

Other spikenards exist, but of different species. The spikes are collected and used in the perfume industry.

Stockwort see Agrimony.

Strychnine *(Strychnos nux-vomica).* This drug is extracted from the seeds of a tree that grows in India and southeast Asia.

Medicinal use in small doses to increase sensitivity, but overdose produces uncontrollable spasms that are fatal unless treated. Poisonous.

Sundew *(Drosera rotundifolia).* Up to 30 cm (12 in). Small, white or pinkish flowers; naked flower stem, basal rosette of leaves that are nearly round, reddish, glandular-hairy, and exude a liquid that traps insects. Found in damp places, usually moorland and general wild areas.

Medicinal use for respiratory ailments and chest problems, including coughs, asthma, and bronchitis. Plant contains an antibiotic that is active against streptococcus.

Used only in small quantities, as it contains irritants.

Sweet Cicely *(Myrrhis odorata* 60-90 cm (2-3 ft) and taller. White flowers in downy umbels. Large, light green leaves, sweet and highly aromatic foliage. Easy to grow, spreading profusely once established.

Culinary use improves all mixtures of herbs; added to salad dressings, soups, root vegetables, and cabbage. Roots can be boiled and eaten. Reduces acidity in fruit.

Tansy *(Tanacetum vulgare)* 30-150 cm (1-5 ft). Golden-yellow flowers in flattened clusters; smooth, dark green leaves divided into segments and toothed; purplish-brown

stem. Cultivated, but also found growing wild.

Can be **poisonous**, even when applied externally. American Indians used as tea to induce abortion.

Tarragon *(Artemisia dracunculus).* French variety

Tansy

grows to 1 m (40 in). Russian variety grows up to 150 cm (5 ft), is tougher, but is not flavorful. Grayish woolly flowers in clusters; graceful, dark green leaves widely spaced on stem. Cultivated best on well-drained land. Culinary use chopped in salad dressings. Sprinkled over salads, in sauces, and main dishes.

Thistle *(Cirsium palustre)* (Marsh Thistle). Up to 150 cm (5 ft). The common tall thistle found in fields and woods and on wet ground, with the familiar purple flower and thorny leaves and stems.

Culinary use of young shoots, with prickles and tough skin removed, in salads or boiled.

Thyme *(Thymus vulgaris)* (Common Thyme) Lemon Thyme *(Thymus citriodorus).* There are other species, but these are the two main ones. Both are low bushes, 10-30 cm (4-12 in), with pale mauve flowers; small leaves, but lemon variety has broader leaves and an unmistakable lemon scent. Can easily be grown in a well-drained sunny location. Suitable for rock-gardens.

Culinary use of warm, clove-like flavor in wide variety of dishes. If used too liberally, may overcome the taste of other herbs.

Medicinal use of tea for coughs and colds. The oil has antiseptic qualities. Overuse may have poisoning effects.

Trefoil see Bird's Foot Trefoil.

Turmeric *(Curcuma longa).* Comes from the dried root of a plant in the ginger family, coming from the tropics.

Culinary use of ground nut with care; has a bitter, gingery taste. Main use in small quantities to give color to foods such as mustards and curries.

Valerian *(Valeriana officinalis)* 100-150 cm (3-5 ft). Numerous small, pale pink flowers in clusters; toothed leaflets, usually unbranched; hairy in parts; roots grow out like a head of hair.

Medicinal use of the roots to overcome insomnia but should not be used without advice and is **addictive.**

Vanilla *(Vanilla planifolia).* Comes from the long pod of a tropical vine. The pods are fermented and cured for six months before marketing. Extract is prepared by mashing pods in alcohol.

89

Watercress

Verbenas Vervain *(Verbena officinalis)* Lemon Verbena *(Lippia citriodora)*. Two different plants, often confused. Vervain is 30-60 cm (1-2 ft); small lilac flowers on long slender spikes; rough and hairy plant with square stems. Lemon verbena is similar in height but has yellowish-green leaves, shiny on upper side, and pale lavender flowers in slender downy clusters. Both plants can be cultivated, but the latter is rather delicate.

Use of vervain tea is supposed to stimulate production of bile and to act as a sedative; also supposed to

clear the sight.

Culinary use of lemon verbena leaves in fruit drinks and salads; lemon-scented. Drunk as a scented tea in Spain.

Viper's Bugloss see Bugloss

Violet Sweet Violet *(Viola odorate)*. Familiar wild violet; violet, white, yellow, or rose-colored flowers; leaves at base; sends out runners along ground. Found wild in hedgerows and the edges of woods.

Medicinal use of whole plant for tea used as a soothing gargle. Tea or syrup made from flowers; root is remedy for coughs.

Watercress *(Nasturitum officinale)*. Stem up to 60 cm (2 ft). Creeping root under water; white flowers. Found everywhere in streams and ditches.

Culinary use in salads. Older leaves have stronger flavor, but wash very carefully as liver fluke eggs may be in hollow stem. High vitamin C content.

Medicinal use of diluted juice for eczema and anemia. Excessive use can lead to kidney problems.

Water Dock see Dock

White Bryony see Bryony

White Horehound see Horehound

White Willow *(Salix alba)*. The familiar tree form of the willow.

Medicinal use of the rough, gray bark to alleviate pain and reduce fever has been known for two thousand years. Bark is collected in spring time and soaked in water.

Wild Pansy see Heartsease

Witch Hazel *(Hamamelis virginiana)*. Deciduous shrub of small tree growing particularly in North America.

Medicinal use of bark and leaves for familiar preparation,

which acts as an antiseptic and general healer both internally and externally. Can be bought at most pharmacies.

Woad (*(Isatis tinctoria)* 30-100 m (1-3 ft). Yellow flowers; lobed leaves growing directly from root; whole plant has greenish-blue sheen.

Used to make traditional dye.

Wood Betony see Betony

Woodruff *(Galium odoratum or Asperula odorata)* 15-30 cm (6-12 in). White star-shaped flowers rising out of dark green whorls of leaves, which are slightly shiny and edged with minute forward-pointing prickles. Found wild, and can be cultivated in a suitably wild habitat.

Culinary use of leaves for enhancing the flavor of drinks and adding a sparkle.

Medicinal use of tea as a stimulant.

Wormwood *(Artemesia absinthium)* 60-120 cm (2-4 ft). Numerous tiny yellow-green rayless flower heads; bushy stems, with leaves having long involved lobes. Found wild along roadsides.

Medicinal use of oil from flowers and leaves as a cardiac stimulant and to remove worms. Tea relieves pain during labor. Pure oil is a poison, and care should be exercised in use.

Yarrow *(Achillei millefolium)* 30-70 cm (12-28 in). Flowers have white rays and yellow disks, arranged in large bunches at top of pithy stem, which is smooth and round. Often found in waste areas, making a colorful display.

Medicinal use of tea from whole herb for lack of appetite and liver problems; also is well known in healing wounds. Fresh juice is supposed to act as a tonic. Extended use may make skin sensitive to light.

Book list

There are a large number of books about herbs. Some concentrate on the medicinal approach, others on the culinary uses. Many call themselves complete when they fall far short of being such, others concentrate more on visual appeal than on factual accuracy or completeness. The following list does not intend to be exhaustive, but suggests books which are worth further attention.

Better Homes and Gardens Vegetables and Herbs,
Meredith.

The Book of Herbs,
Dorothy Hall, Scribners.

Collecting Roots and Herbs for Fun and Profit,
Martha Sherwood, Contemporary Books.

The Concise Herbal Encyclopedia,
Donald Law, St. Martins.

A Cook's Guide to Growing Herbs, Greens, and Aromatics,
Millie Owen, Knopf.

Culinary and Salad Herbs,
Eleanor Rohde, Dover.

Gardening with Herbs for Flavor and Fragrance,
Helen M. Fox, Dover.

The Golden Age of Herbs and Herbalists,
Rosetta E. Clarkson, Dover.

Growing Herbs in Pots,
John Brimer, Simon and Schuster.

The Herb and Spice Book for Kids,
Alice Siegel and Margo McLoone, Holt, Rinehart and Winston.

The Herb Book,
John Lust (ed.), Bantam.

Herb Grower's Guide: Cooking, Spicing and Lore,
John Prenis, Running Press.

Herbs and the Earth,
Henry Beston, Doubleday.

Herbs to Grow Indoors,
Adelma Simmons, Hawthorn.

A Heritage of Herbs: History, Early Gardening, and Old Recipes,
Bertha P. Reppert, Stackpole.

How to Grow Herbs and Salad Greens Indoors,
Joan W. Meschter, Popular Library.

Let Herbs Do It,
Virginia W. Bentley, Houghton, Mifflin.

The Magic of Herbs,
David Conway, Dutton.

A Modern American Herbal,
Chester B. Dugdale, A.S. Barnes.

Modern Encyclopedia of Herbs,
Joseph Kodaus, Prentice-Hall.

The Time-Life Encyclopedia of Gardening Series,
Time-Life.

A Wonder of Herbs,
Sigmund Lavine, Dodd.

Index of Latin names

Ilex vomitoria, Cassina
Indigofera sumatrana, Indigo
Inula helenium, Elecampane
Iris florentina, Iris Florentina
Isatis tinctoria, Woad
Jasminum officinale, Jasmine
Juniperus communis, Juniper
Lactuca virosa, Lettuce
Laurus nobilis, Bay
Lavendula officinalis etc.,
    Lavender
Lawsonia inermis, Henna
Ligusticum officinalis, Lovage
Lippia citriodora, Lemon
    Verbena
Linum usitatissimum, Linseed
Lonicera periclymenum,
    Honeysuckle
Lotus corniculatus, Bird's Foot
    Trefoil
Malva sylvestris rotundifolia,
    Mallow
Mandragora officinarum,
    Mandrake
Maranta arundinacea,
    Arrowroot
Marrubium vulgare, Horehound
Matricaria chamomilla,
    Chamomile
Melissa officinalis, Balm
Mentha aquatica, Water Mint
Mentha citrata, Eau-de-
    Cologne Mint
Mentha piperita, Black
    Peppermint
Mentha piperita officinalis,
    White Peppermint
Mentha pulegium, Pennyroyal
Mentha rotundifolia, Apple
    Mint
Mentha rotundifolia, Bowles
    variety, Bowles Mint
Mentha rotundifolia variegata,
    Pineapple Mint
*Mentha spicata and Mentha
    crispa*, Curley Mint
Mentha viridis, Spearmint
Mimosa acacia, Mimosa
Monarda didyma, Bergamot

Red
Morus nigra, Mulberry
Myristica fragans, Nutmeg
Myrrhis odorata, Sweet Cicely
Nardostarchys jatamausi,
    Spikenard
Nasturtium officinale,
    Watercress
Nepeta cataria, Catnip
Nepta hedracea, Ground Ivy
Ocimum basilicum, Basil
Olea europaea, Olive
Ophioglossum vulgatum,
    Adder's Tongue
*Origanum majorana onites
    vulgare*, Marjoram
Panax schin-seng, Ginseng
Papaver somninferum, Opium
    Poppy
Paeonia officinalis, Peony
Petastites vulgaris, Butterbur
Pimenta officinalis, Allspice
Pimpinella anisum, Anise
Piper cubeba, Cubeb
Piper nigrum, Pepper
Plantago major, Plantain
Podophyllum pelatum,
    Mandrake
Polygonum bistorta, Bistort
Portulaca oleracea, Purslane
Potentilla reptans, Cinquefoil
Primula officinalis, Primrose
Primula veris, Cowslip
Prunus amygdalus, Almond
Prunus spinosa, Blackthorne
Quercus robur, Oak
Ranunculus repens, Creeping
    Buttercup
Rosa canina, Rose Hips
Rosa rugosa, Wild Rose
Rosa rubiginora, Sweetbriar
Rosmarinus officinalis,
    Rosemary
Rubiaceae, many sp. Cinchona
Rubia tinctorum, Madder
Rubus fruticosus, Blackberry
Rumex acetosa, Sorrel
Rumex hydrolapathum, Dock
Ruscus aculeatus, Butcher's

Broom
Ruta graveolens, Rue
Saliva officinalis, Sage
Salix alba, White Willow
Sambucus nigra, Elder
Sanguisorba minor, Burnet
Satureja hortensis, Summer
    Savory
Satureia montana, Winter
    Savory
Scutellaria lateriflora, Skullcap
Senecio jacobaea, Ragwort
Senecio vulgaris, Groundsel
Sesamum indicum, Sesame
    seeds
Solanum nigrum, Deadly
    nightshade
Solidago virgaurea, Solidago
Sphagnum, Sphagnum Moss
Stachys officinalis, Betony
Stelleria media, Chickweed
Strychnos nux-vomica,
    Strychnine
Symphytum officinale, Comfrey
Tanacetum vulgare, Tansy
Taraxacum officinale, Dandelion
Thymus citriodorus, Lemon
    Thyme
Thymus vulgaris, Thyme
Trifolium pratense, Clover
Trigonella ornithopodioides,
    Fenugreek
Tropaeolum majus, Nasturtium
Tulipa silvestris, Wild Tulip
Turnera aphrodisiaca, Damiana
Tussilago farfara, Coltsfoot
Urtica dioica, Nettle
Valerian officinalis, Valerian
Vanilla planifolia, Vanilla
Verbascum thapsiforme,
    Mullein
Verbena officinalis, Verbena
Vetiveria zizanioides,
    Khus-Khus
Vinca major, Periwinkle
Viola odorata, Violet
Viola tricolour, Heartsease
Viscum album, Mistletoe
Zingiber officinale, Ginger

Index

Credits

Artists
Pat Lenander
Vanessa Luff

Photographs
A-Z Collection Ltd.:
   Contents, 27, 29, 40.
American Spice Trade
   Assoc.: 18

Bibliothèque Nationale: 12
Bodleian Library, Oxford:
   Contents, 11
Paul Forrester: 57, 61, 63, 68
Michael Holford: 34
Hubertus Kanns/Barnaby's
   Picture Library: 31
Victor Kennett: 32
Mansell Collection: 22

National Gallery: 9
Radio Times Hulton Picture
   Library: contents, 8, 10, 23
G. R. Roberts, Nelson,
   New Zealand: 45
Roman Picture Library: 11
J. Sainsbury Ltd.: 9
Victoria & Albert Museum:
   17, 19